250 QUESTIONS FOR STARTING A NONPROFIT

MARTIN STEPHENS

Aadamsmedia

Avon, Massachusetts

Published by
Adams Media, a division of F+W Media, Inc.
57 Littlefield Street, Avon, MA 02322. U.S.A.
www.adamsmedia.com

Contains material adapted and abridged from *The Everything® Guide to Starting and Running a Nonprofit* by Jim Goettler, copyright © 2010 by F+W Media, Inc., ISBN 10: 1-4405-0015-0, ISBN 13: 978-1-4405-0015-2.

ISBN 10: 1-4405-8454-0
ISBN 13: 978-1-4405-8454-1
eISBN 10: 1-4405-8455-9
eISBN 13: 978-1-4405-8455-8

Printed in the United States of America.

10 9 8 7 6 5 4 3 2 1

This book is available at quantity discounts for bulk purchases.
For information, please call 1-800-289-0963.

CONTENTS

INTRODUCTION

Many people are undergoing economic hardship. The "Great Recession" had long-lasting effects on the finances of almost everyone in the country. There's a huge income gap between the haves and the have-nots in the United States. The college graduating class of 2014 had the highest student loan debt ever. And a recent study revealed that one in three Americans is not only in debt, but is also behind on their payments.

People need help, and they need it right now.

Fortunately, for as long as there has been hardship, there have been people who want to help. That's where nonprofits come in. Nonprofits take on roles that were once handled by government agencies, or step in when government intervention is not enough. They can do everything from feeding the homeless, to building houses after natural disasters, to funding arts and music programs. Starting a nonprofit is a noble goal, but there are many complicated steps to navigate along the way—steps with which this book will help you.

Sometimes it's hard to know the right questions you need to ask to get started. This book asks—and answers!—them for you. It will guide you through the basic steps of setting up a nonprofit organization: crafting a mission statement, finding staff members, and selecting the members of your board. It will also give you some ideas on how to go about one of the most important tasks of a nonprofit: fundraising. Finally, you'll be taken through the complicated steps of becoming an official nonprofit: filing your articles of incorporation, crafting a business plan, and filling out the application for federal nonprofit status.

Obtaining nonprofit status for your organization is a major accomplishment that helps assure that your organization will be able to continue your charitable good works for years to come, even after you're no longer involved. However, the tax-exempt status that comes with being a federally recognized nonprofit is a valuable commodity, one the IRS fiercely protects. At each step of forming your nonprofit, you must be careful in how you write your bylaws, how you conduct yourself, and how you handle your money, in order to avoid jeopardizing your nonprofit status.

In addition to answering all your questions about forming a nonprofit, in the back of the book you'll find sample Articles of Incorporation, bylaws, and job descriptions, to help you get started when crafting these crucial documents. It's important to check what your individual state requires when dealing with any official documents. Some states have their own forms, and some states have no forms at all.

This book is not meant to be the only resource you consult; rather it's a jumping-off point for you to gain a basic understanding about starting a nonprofit organization and obtaining nonprofit status. Later on, as you're filing your paperwork, use it as a valuable reference guide to make sure you're meeting every requirement.

Starting a nonprofit is a great adventure that is sure to be challenging but also rewarding. Good luck, enjoy the journey, and start asking questions!

PART **I**

Getting Started

Chapter 1

THE BASICS

#1. Why nonprofits?

When problems and issues arise in communities, the people in those communities come together to fix them. Often such movements are led by organizers, whose job it is to bring together like-minded people. For any group of people to make lasting change, there must be some form of organization, a structure that will enable them to raise money, set an agenda, and carry out tasks in service of that agenda.

This is what a nonprofit does.

If you're involved in a nonprofit, you aren't doing this organizing to make a profit as you might if you were working in a corporation. What's important to you is the *goal* of the nonprofit. Your passion may be for the local community or it may be about a national or global entity. Whatever the case, your nonprofit brings together people with shared interests who want to accomplish something. To that end, they've formed a legal entity in which all profits are returned to the organization and the community it serves.

No one questions the need for many of the services that nonprofits or charities assume as necessary for healthy, vibrant communities, so the government grants a lot of leeway in recognition of the sacrifices that individuals involved in nonprofits are willing to make. The government understands that nonprofits exist because of their members' passion for a cause.

However, regulations governing every aspect of forming and operating a nonprofit organization have become complex. Books such as this one can help you understand and cope with this mountain of rules; as well, you can draw on the expertise of business professionals.

#2. **What is a nonprofit?**

To understand fully what a nonprofit corporation is, it helps first to understand what a for-profit corporation is. A corporation is a unique legal entity recognized by state and federal governments as completely separate from the people who own it. Corporations are viewed as though they were people, with many of the same rights and privileges, although technically many of the companies only exist on paper.

For-profit corporations have five essential components:

1. They may have "limited liability," meaning investors in the corporation can only lose (or are only liable for) the amount of money they have invested, rather than potentially losing everything they own.
2. They maintain a "continuity of existence," which means that the corporation can literally exist forever, well beyond the lifetimes of the founders or current owners.
3. They offer an "ease of ownership transfer" through the sale of shares, rather than selling the actual business.
4. They have the ability to raise money or capital through expanded ownership. In other words, if more shares are sold or more partners are brought in, there is no limit to the amount of money that can be raised—and of course, lost.
5. They offer shareholders the ability to profit from the growth of the business through the increased value of

their shares, when shares are sold on the open market, or through the payment of dividends based on the profit the corporation has generated.

Nonprofit corporations share many of these characteristics. However, unlike for-profit corporations, in which individual owners, partners, or shareholders may personally benefit from the organization, in a nonprofit corporation no individual may directly benefit from any "profit" generated by the organization. Rather, the money generally considered "profit" must be turned back into the organization to continue its work.

Nonprofit organizations can and do make money, although, as stated previously, this money must be returned to the corporation. Nonprofits may also hire staff, engage private consultants, and operate as does any other corporation; the important distinction is that salaries or fees of employees must be established as set amounts rather than—as in a for-profit company—based on the corporation's financial performance. A sliding-scale compensation structure that depends on the success of the organization would place employees, especially officers, in the position of directly benefiting from the organization. This would be contrary to the tax code and in all probability cause the nonprofit to lose its tax-exempt status.

#3. **What are the three main types of nonprofits?**

There are three main categories of nonprofit corporations. Under these three categories are more familiar subcategories:

1. The **public benefit corporation** includes the generally understood charitable organizations and social welfare organizations such as those with a 501(c)(3) or a 501(c)(4) classification.
2. The **mutual benefit corporation**, which is not public, might include groups such as homeowners' associations and private foundations.

3. The great **other**, which includes fraternal societies, labor organizations, farm bureaus, social clubs, veterans' organizations, cemetery companies, credit unions, and the many other organizations listed under section 501(c) of the Internal Revenue Service code.

#4.   What is the difference between a 501(c)(3) and a 501(c)(4) organization?

First, let's look at the similarities. Both are exempt from paying federal income tax; both must be operated as nonprofits; and are restricted from allowing any individual or shareholder to benefit financially from the work of the organization. In fact, because those particular rules are so similar, any organization that qualifies for 501(c)(3) status also qualifies for 501(c)(4) status.

A 501(c)(4) meets three criteria:

1. The group is a civic league or organization that is not organized for profit but is operated exclusively for the promotion of social welfare.
2. The group is a local association of employees, the membership of which is limited to the employees of a designated person or persons in a particular municipality.
3. The net earnings of the group are devoted exclusively to charitable, educational, or recreational purposes.

You'll note some similarities to the requirements for the 501(c)(3) status—in particular that the group is, in fact, operating as a not-for-profit. The big differences involve what types of activities the group plans to undertake, with particular focus on political activities.

Whereas a 501(c)(3) is not permitted to advocate for a political candidate or ballot initiative, a 501(c)(4) may do so, as long as the activities fall within its primary purpose. The tradeoff is that contributions to a 501(c)(4) are tax deductible only if the organization is a government agency or is involved in public service. Otherwise, contributions may not be deducted from the personal income tax of the contributor.

If you meet all the other requirements pertaining to both classifications, are not planning to be directly involved in political campaigns, will not be lobbying to a large degree, and plan to solicit tax-deductible donations, consider applying for the 501(c)(3) status.

If, on the other hand, you meet all the other requirements pertaining to both classifications but *do* plan on being actively involved in political campaigns, will be conducting extensive lobbying, and understand that your contributors will generally not be able to deduct those contributions, then consider the 501(c)(4). Some groups have formed two separate tax-exempt organizations, allowing one part of their organization (the c-3) to fully comply with the lobbying and campaigning restrictions and focus solely on the educational component, while the other (the c-4) conducts political outreach and activities.

#5. What are the federal nonprofit categories?

It's likely that a 501(c)(3) or a 501(c)(4) classification will be all that is needed for your nonprofit. However, there may be situations where it may be advantageous for you to apply for another determination in addition to a primary classification. As your organization grows to maturity and everyone involved becomes comfortable with the opportunities and the limitations of your tax-exempt status—or if you find your operations are expanding beyond your original mission—you should seek other exemptions, or perhaps form another organization.

The following table shows the current federal nonprofit categories. Each has precise rules governing how funds may be collected, whether contributors may also claim tax deductions for their donations, who may or may not participate in the organization, how money may be spent, and exactly what kinds of reporting are required to maintain nonprofit status.

Types of Nonprofit Organizations

Section of IRS Code	Type of Organization
501(c)(1)	Corporations organized under an act of Congress
501(c)(2)	Title-holding companies
501(c)(3)	Religious, charitable, educational groups
501(c)(4)	Groups that promote social welfare
501(c)(5)	Labor, agriculture associations
501(c)(6)	Business leagues
501(c)(7)	Social and recreational clubs
501(c)(8)	Fraternal beneficiary societies
501(c)(9)	Voluntary employees' beneficiary associations
501(c)(10)	Domestic fraternal societies
501(c)(11)	Teachers' retirement funds
501(c)(12)	Benevolent life insurance associations
501(c)(13)	Cemetery companies
501(c)(14)	Credit unions (not established by Congress)
501(c)(15)	Mutual insurance companies
501(c)(16)	Corporations to finance crop operations
501(c)(17)	Supplemental unemployment benefit trusts
501(c)(18)	Employee funded pension trusts
501(c)(19)	War veterans' organizations
501(c)(20)	Group legal services organizations
501(c)(21)	Black lung trusts
501(c)(22)	Withdrawal liability payment fund
501(c)(23)	Veterans' organizations (created before 1880)
501(c)(24)	Only one organization, Spring Prairie Hutterian Brethren Inc., in Hawley, Minnesota, is registered as a 501(c)(24) entity as a special trust under the Employee Retirement Income Security Act of 1974
501(c)(25)	Title holding corporations or trusts with multiple parents
501(c)(26)	State-sponsored organizations providing health coverage for high-risk individuals
501(c)(27)	State-sponsored workers' compensation reinsurance organizations

501(d)	Religious and apostolic associations
501(e)	Cooperative hospital service organizations
501(f)	Cooperative service organizations of operating educational organizations
501(k)	Child-care organizations
501(n)	Charitable risk pools
521(a)	Farmers' cooperative associations
527	Political organizations

#6. Do I need an MBA to start a nonprofit?

To a large degree, the founders of nonprofit organizations do not come from the business community. Although a formal business education or background is expected when starting a for-profit corporation, it has been acceptable not to have that background when starting a nonprofit since the earliest days of public charities. The government understands that nonprofits exist because their members are passionate about a cause. As a result, the lack of business skills is occasionally overlooked.

However, a growing number of business professionals are stepping up to offer their assistance in starting nonprofits. If you do not have a business background, don't worry. There is an entire support system of MBAs to show you the ropes.

#7. How should a nonprofit first engage the community?

Being proactive in your interactions with your neighbors and city officials is essential for your nonprofit's success. Where and how you choose to set up your organization's office and operations may affect your neighbors. You may never have given traffic and parking a second thought until now, but they are issues every organization with public or walk-in traffic comes to know well. Parking is the biggest source of problems in neighborhoods where a new organization sets up.

Every time you hold a meeting or a public event, your attendees will park in the street or in a spot that was "reserved." If you have access to off-street parking, you are well ahead of the game, but the vast majority of groups do not have that option. Engaging the immediate community so that everyone understands what you are planning to do will help neutralize much of the opposition and fear of the unknown that plagues many nonprofits.

#8.   **How does the Citizens United ruling affect nonprofits?**

In January 2008, at the height of Hillary Clinton's presidential campaign, Citizens United, a nonprofit organization, released a ninety-minute documentary titled *Hillary: The Movie*. The film expressed opinions about whether or not Senator Clinton, a candidate for the Democratic presidential nomination, was fit for the presidency. The nonprofit produced advertisements promoting the film and wanted to show them on broadcast and cable television and video-on-demand. To pay for these, Citizens United planned to use its general treasury funds. (General treasury funds are all of the assets of an organization that are spent as a normal part of doing business.)

Until this time, federal law prohibited corporations and unions from directly spending their general treasury funds on "electioneering communications" or on speech that expressly advocated the election or defeat of a candidate close to an election; most everyone agreed that *Hillary* did so. Concerned that spending money in support of the production and distribution of the movie close to an election day might be found to be illegal, Citizens United sued the Federal Communications Commission (FCC) to prevent it from enforcing this law.

The case finally made its way to the U.S. Supreme Court. In January 2010 the Court ruled that corporations and unions have the same political speech rights as individuals under the First Amendment. It found no reason to prohibit corporations and unions from using their general treasury funds to make election-related independent expenditures close to an election or at any time they chose.

So what does this mean for your nonprofit? The Citizens United ruling does not impact a 501(c)(3) nonprofit. Regardless of the changes in election law, the federal tax law that prohibits 501(c)(3)s from supporting or opposing candidates still applies. A 501(c)(3) still cannot endorse candidates or make independent expenditures suggesting who is the "better" candidate.

What the ruling does do, though, is complicate the environment in which many nonprofits operate. It opens the doors to corporate interests, whose policies may be at odds with those of the nonprofit. For example, if a nonprofit organization conducts classes for schoolchildren in nature conservation, advocating practices opposed by a corporation, unlimited corporate money can now be spent to defeat those practices.

However, the ruling also means that your nonprofit can also be a vehicle for political advocacy. Nonprofit 501(c)(4) or 501(c)(6) organizations can make independent expenditures furthering political advocacy using the organization's general funds to support or oppose candidates for the U.S. House, the Senate, and the presidency, as well as state legislative and judicial offices. Previously, these independent expenditures for political purposes had to be made through political action committees (PACs) using voluntary donations, rather than general treasury funds.

Over all, the Citizens United ruling opens up tremendous opportunities for groups that do not have the 501(c)(3) determination to become more actively involved in the political life of their communities. This decision may, in fact, help further the overall mission of many nonprofit organizations as well as increase the impact of your group on your community.

#9.   **What kind of time commitment does a nonprofit require?**

One of the overlooked elements involved in starting a non-profit organization, especially a community-based one that will rely heavily on volunteers, is the time commitment for everyone involved. In a mature organization with paid staff, everyone has set hours. When you are relying on volunteers, the scheduling depends on the other things in their lives. The time people can commit to the organization will, necessarily, often take a lower priority. However, with a combination of planning and compassion your volunteers will find ways to balance their nonprofit activity with their other commitments. Of course, if you are one of the main organizers or a member of the board of directors, the new organization will become your constant mental companion.

As much as you may think you can do everything, you can't! You will need to become comfortable asking other people to take on more responsibilities if you believe they are up to speed on whatever they're doing.

As the organization grows, it is essential to ensure that members step back when they are overworked or are no longer fully engaged. Encourage yourself or others to take time to recharge the batteries and return fully refreshed and able to handle the responsibilities of the group.

Chapter 2

NETWORKING WITHIN THE COMMUNITY

#10. Where should I set up my office?

It's essential that your office reflect your relationship with the community. That means, of course, that it needs to be located *in* the community, in a place where people from the neighborhood feel comfortable coming.

Consider such questions as access to public transportation, ease of parking (always a big issue!), and safety both in and around the office. You also should evaluate whether the space is adequate for your needs. Although the nonprofit may grow and need more space in the future, it would be best if you didn't have to move for at least a couple of years. Build in some growth room to your first office.

#11. When should I first interact with leaders of the community?

It's important to meet with local political leaders and introduce yourself to personnel in your city and county administrative offices before you need them. This shows everyone that you are serious about working with the community, even those who may have reservations about your plans. This is an area where your skill as an organizer who is comfortable meeting with strangers is going to help.

Much of organizing a nonprofit comes down to establishing and building relationships with not only those people who are supportive of your plans but also those who oppose your organization. If your plans involve zoning or occupancy regulations, all your skills as an organizer and negotiator will come into play. By working with—rather than confronting—local review boards or citizen groups, you should be fine.

#12.   How do I first assess the local media?

Begin by looking at the traditional forms of local media: radio, the daily newspaper, and local television, including any cable access channels. Are there writers at the paper who are sympathetic to your project? How about radio personalities? Is there a nonprofit station that not only accepts community groups but also actively encourages them with free airtime or production assistance for public service announcements (PSAs)?

One of the first things to do is create some PSAs that you can give to these media outlets. A great tool you can use to produce PSAs is a widely available software program called Audacity. Audacity turns your computer into a mini-recording studio, able to produce broadcast-quality audio files. Audacity is remarkably intuitive and can be used with only a little practice; the same can be said for other basic recording/editing programs.

If you don't already have a local media list, put one together that includes all the outlets, their general contact information, and a rough tracking of both supportive and critical articles they have put out over the past year. You want to get a good sense of where you will find both support and criticism. With that understanding, you will be able to better present the pros and cons of incorporating as a nonprofit.

#13.   How do I introduce myself to the media?

If there is a community radio or television station, that should be your first stop. Introduce yourself to the station manager and news director as soon as it is practical. Without the start-up funding necessary to personally contact every individual in your area, learning to work with the media is your best way to reach the largest number of people and will provide a direct means of communicating with your supporters throughout the region. Keep in mind that the people who work in community media need you to help provide content for their programming just as much as you need them to help publicize your activities.

If your organization is statewide or even nationwide in scope, the local broadcast and print outlets can provide direct access to a national audience with the flip of a switch. Over the past decade, new networks serving millions of people have been established; you need to become acquainted with these networks and plan to use them.

As you access available resources of the media, don't overlook the Internet mailing lists called *listservs*. Some of these undoubtedly include groups that have the same focus as you do. Now is the time to document every media resource and develop a file listing every element they have that is applicable to your needs.

#14.   How do I introduce myself to the local business community?

Start with the local chamber of commerce and other business groups. News of your organization has probably already been circulating, so take the initiative and request an informal meeting with these groups. This meeting will help you position yourself for future cooperation. Create a simple brochure using a desktop publishing program. Have copies available at every meeting you attend, and your crucial first impression as a well-planned, successful venture will be a positive one.

Take the initiative and offer to meet with local businesses. You will encounter people in your community with whom you might never have otherwise met, which will allow you to form potentially advantageous relationships.

#15. How should I use Facebook to reach out to the community?

In the past few years, social media has completely transformed online communication. Users can directly contact hundreds—if not thousands—of people with an immediacy never seen before. Fortunately, the most popular systems have been designed to allow users with minimal technical know-how to make use of the environment fairly quickly.

Facebook (*www.facebook.com*) allows you to freely interact with others. While there are many more uses for Facebook, you'll find this aspect of it the most useful for your nonprofit.

In addition to providing a means for people to stay in touch, Facebook also lets organizations have a public, free presence on the web with a potential worldwide viewership. How many people visit your nonprofit's Facebook page will be determined by how aggressive and active you are in promoting it. As friends become part of your nonprofit's network, potential visits can increase exponentially within days or weeks.

Unless people have their memberships set to receive updates via e-mail or text, they must go to your Facebook page to see what activities you are posting. As many people are simply unable to track everything going on within their many groups and many friends, cross-promotion becomes very important.

#16. **How should I use Twitter to reach out to the community?**

While Facebook relies on overlapping, interconnected circles of associates or acquaintances to create the huge networks that are the basis of that system, Twitter (*www.twitter.com*) allows a lot of people to be alerted simultaneously to the same event.

The people who are following you can be notified of a special event you are presenting, meetings they may want to attend, or anything else the organization feels necessary to communicate to its membership and followers. You can also use your tweets, the 140-character messages transmitted via the Twitter network, to drive traffic to your Facebook page or to your website.

Although Twitter is usually associated with cell phones that have a data plan, it can also be accessed from any computer, making communication directly to your membership an easy process.

#17. **How should I use LinkedIn to reach out to the community?**

The third system that should form the core of your social media activities is LinkedIn (*www.linkedin.com*). LinkedIn was not designed for the massive volume of Facebook or the immediacy of Twitter. It's a networking tool for use by professionals interested in connecting with others in their field.

LinkedIn is not limited to any one profession or area of interest, which makes it a terrific tool for the organizer of a non-profit. As users indicate their general areas of expertise, locating other people with a shared interest, or professionals you may need for consulting purposes, is just a few clicks away.

In addition to the networking LinkedIn provides, it is also a good means of gathering ideas and unique perspectives presented by other users who regularly post what they are doing and why. The system provides both direct and indirect e-mail exchanges through their e-mail relay service.

People who sign up and use LinkedIn regularly welcome communication. Feel free to send a note to individuals sharing your interest and to those with whom you feel collaboration may be possible.

#18.   How should I use Flickr to reach out to the community?

If your organization's activities are visually appealing, or if you have photographers at every event you present, consider using a social media site expressly designed to both store and show photographs—Flickr (*www.flickr.com*). Flickr is owned by Yahoo! and will require a Yahoo! account to use, but as with all the other major social media platforms, it allows and encourages logging in from other accounts (i.e., Facebook or Twitter). In turn, this makes it easy to reference back to those sites, as well as have your homepage clearly visible with an active link.

Flickr is not a site for detailed explanations of your organization or a place to publicize the minutes of your last board meeting. It's a place to share photographs of volunteers working on a project, or your table at a neighborhood street fair, or anything you feel presents your group in the best possible light for all to see. The general public—and in particular, potential donors—always appreciates seeing photographs of your activities as they consider helping you further your mission.

As with the other forms of social media, a basic account is free. The systems receive their income from advertising revenue.

#19.   **How should I use YouTube to reach out to the community?**

YouTube (*www.youtube.com*) is a must-have tool for your online activities. Producing videos for YouTube does not require any more equipment than is generally included in newer computers (namely, a webcam and a microphone). As your interest and finances allow, you may get more sophisticated equipment, but it is not necessary to get started; in fact, many individuals and organizations never progress past that simple stock equipment.

Your organization can create its own channel and begin to upload videos you have created of your volunteers sharing their stories, your special events, your meetings, and anything else you think is important. When your nonprofit is cross-promoted through the other online services, people will understand your entire story and begin to share the passion necessary for them to want to participate. As with the other forms of social media, consider using the videos for general outreach and to share information, but also to drive traffic back to your website and that ever-important donation button.

#20.   **Should I reach out to other groups in my community?**

Yes! Unless you are in a small town or live in a rural area, it is likely that there are other organizations in the region working on similar issues. Some of the organizations may be informal associations. Some may be incorporated as state nonprofits, and others may have obtained their federal nonprofit status. Regardless of their legal status or exactly how they have chosen to organize themselves, they may be doing similar work and could be of tremendous help to you and your organization.

When setting out to meet the directors or board members of similar groups, plan ahead and strategize about exactly what you hope to get out of the meeting and what you are able to offer. Especially when discretionary funds in a community are tight, you need to be willing to collaborate to eliminate any fear of competition.

Just as many professions and skilled trades have formed unique associations and guilds over the years, so too have nonprofit organizations joined forces to share resources and general support. Seek out these organizations well before you formally incorporate or apply for your nonprofit status. Many of these organizations—whether they are arts, cultural, or social service groups—have publications and websites for their members as well as more general information for nonmembers.

Guest memberships are often available for new organizations. Taking advantage of this avenue allows you to get a sense of what these organizations can offer and what your peers are doing.

Chapter 3

THE FIRST MEETING

#21. Should I publicize my nonprofit's first meeting?

Avoid publicizing an initial meeting. It is far better to make personal invitations by telephone or e-mail to people who have already expressed an interest in working together. There will be plenty of time to invite the community into the organization once your group is more established.

#22. How should I set up for the first meeting?

Arrive ten to fifteen minutes early to turn on the lights, arrange chairs, set out snacks, and get ready to welcome invitees. Print a sign-in sheet with spaces for names, telephone numbers, and e-mail addresses. If you are drawing from a larger geographic area, leave space for a mailing address so you know where people live, even though you'll probably communicate almost exclusively by e-mail. This sign-in sheet can help the person taking minutes remember who said what, and it will also serve as the beginnings of a contact sheet, the core of your organization's database.

If the meeting space does not have a chalkboard, bring a portable easel and a large paper tablet or whiteboard. Print out copies of any background information that was sent out earlier, including a draft agenda if one was prepared. Try to schedule the meeting for early evening and let everyone know it will last no longer than two hours.

#23.   How should I structure our first meeting?

Approach the first meeting with an open mind. Even though the attendees probably have been making plans based on their notions of how the group should function, the purpose of an initial meeting is to encourage the discussion of everyone's ideas.

The first step is introductions. Ask each attendee to take a minute to say why he or she is interested in the group, how they learned of the meeting, and how they make a living. This is a not-too-subtle way of finding out what each person might bring to the organization.

Next, focus the rest of the meeting on your group's goals and how you will achieve them. The facilitator should guide the discussion as the group works through what the attendees want to see happen. You can base your agenda on the questions in this chapter. Create a plan of action so you can follow up after the meeting. This plan should outline the steps that everyone chooses for moving forward and designate people to take on specific tasks. The facilitator may have to ask for volunteers or ask attendees to take on certain tasks.

#24.   What are the limitations of a nonprofit?

Your first organizing meeting is an excellent time to discuss the limitations of applying for nonprofit status and the requirements involved in annual reporting to the IRS and to your state. Everyone concerned with the actual organizing must understand the ramifications of becoming a nonprofit and how it may directly affect him or her. The law prohibits any personal gain from nonprofit work. This means monetary compensation cannot depend on a sliding-scale model that would make payment directly contingent on the success of the organization. Similarly, the core organizers may want to be compensated for the work they do. Such work must be compensated at the fair market value; organizers should not be paid simply for being on the board. Board members may be reimbursed for travel or miscellaneous expenses related to their attendance at board meetings.

A nonprofit is restricted to its purpose in everything it does. Taxes may result if the group chooses to undertake an activity that falls outside its tax-exempt purpose.

#25. **What are the reporting requirements for a nonprofit?**

Although as a federally recognized tax-exempt organization you do not have to pay federal income tax, you must make a detailed financial report to the IRS using Form 990. These forms are available for anyone who wants to see exactly what funds your organization garnered over the past year and where that money went.

Most states also have a requirement that all corporations submit a report of their annual meeting. These reports are not complicated, but they must be sent in every year for the entire life of the organization.

Failure to submit the state or federal reports will cause real trouble for your organization. In extreme cases, your tax-exempt status may be revoked and your corporation closed. A recent decision by the IRS determined that any organization that fails to submit its Form 990 for three years in a row will have its nonprofit status revoked. They are serious about the reporting requirements and you should be as well.

At your initial meeting, you need to decide if you are prepared to take on the long-term responsibility that comes with filing for tax-exempt status.

#26. What is the 20 percent rule, and how does it affect my nonprofit?

For many organizations considering whether to apply for federal tax-exempt status, the rule strictly governing the political activities of a 501(c)(3) nonprofit can be a huge issue. Even organizations that might never consider themselves "political" in any traditional sense must be aware of the rules and adhere to them. There are many situations in which candidates for public office, ballot initiatives, or pending legislation might directly affect your organization and its mission, so this will always be an area that needs attention.

As part of becoming a 501(c)(3) organization, you agreed not to participate directly in political campaigns. Be careful that your organization does not appear to be directly involved in any political campaign. If this occurs, your status will be in jeopardy.

With this said, the 20 percent rule allows a 501(c)(3) nonprofit to spend up to 20 percent of its tax-exempt operating budget on lobbying efforts, although never on advocacy for a particular candidate or ballot initiative. These restrictions do not limit the individuals within your organization. They can work for candidates or campaign for initiatives, but as a 501(c)(3) organization, you agreed the nonprofit would not be involved with any campaign for office or any ballot issue. However, as an organization, you may be involved in general voter education about issues that are relevant to your group, as long as all points of view are presented. You can host forums with candidates or initiative sponsors or opponents, but you may not advocate for one side.

#27. What are the political rules for 501(c)(4) organizations?

If it becomes apparent during your discussion that your group might want a higher level of political involvement, you may want to consider becoming a 501(c)(4) organization.

A 501(c)(4) organization adheres to a different set of rules when it comes to political activity. Although there is no prohibition on advocating for any particular candidate or ballot initiative, a group may only do so if the advocacy is not the group's primary purpose. A 501(c)(4) may, however, spend unlimited funds on general lobbying efforts without jeopardizing its tax-exempt status. It is not bound by the 20 percent rule (see Question #26), but the money spent on direct political campaigning (as opposed to lobbying) may become taxable.

To a casual observer, the difference may not be apparent, but it is substantial. As a publicly supported charity that receives contributions that are tax-deductible, a 501(c)(3) is held to the highest standard with regard to interference in the political process. A 501(c)(4) is still exempt from federal corporate taxes, but contributors do not deduct the money they donate from their income taxes, so advocacy for a cause or issue is permitted.

If an organization obtains its 501(c)(3) status and then violates the restriction on lobbying activities or involvement in political activities and loses its status, it will not be able to qualify later for the 501(c)(4) status.

#28.   Should the organization hire a tax lawyer?

When combining ever-changing state and federal nonprofit tax laws with start-up nonprofit corporations, a long-term relationship with a lawyer who understands your organization and stays up-to-date with changes in tax law can be essential. Be sure to evaluate your planning from a legal perspective so both your organization and the lawyer you choose make the best use of everyone's time. Someone in the group might already know a lawyer who is willing to help (or be a lawyer herself), but if not, seek referrals from other small nonprofit organizations in your immediate area to find a tax lawyer you can trust.

#29.   **What is the twenty-seven month rule and how should the group plan to use it?**

You can incorporate as soon as your organizational documents are ready and you identify the board of directors, which can happen soon after your initial meeting. However, there is a built-in window of twenty-seven months from the time you incorporate until you need to file your IRS Form 1023, the application for tax-exempt status. During this period, your organization should take shape, both internally and within your community. Use the time to identify potential contributors and establish all programs and outreach elements. Start getting media coverage, establishing various committees, and operating as a fully functioning corporation. Before you receive federal recognition, you will be liable for any federal corporate taxes if you generate a level of income requiring it.

The time between your formal incorporation and application for tax-exempt status is designed to allow your organization to come into its own. Acquaint your community or service area with your planned work and answer any questions people have. Use this time to gear up to your full potential; don't hold off on your operations until you apply for a tax exemption. Make use of the people who gathered for your initial meeting. You can generate media coverage, contact major sponsors, and do everything a nonprofit would do.

Your corporate tax exemption will be retroactive to the time of your formal incorporation, but during the window between incorporation and the receipt of your determination letter granting tax-exempt status, you may be responsible for federal taxes. Once again, you may want to seek the advice of a tax professional to determine how best to proceed in your unique situation.

Chapter 4

THE BOARD OF DIRECTORS

#30. How many members should serve on the initial board?

Many states specify the minimum number of board members, and the respective incorporation documents should indicate this number. Generally, on the initial board, three people will be sufficient. Remember to specify that number in your bylaws as the minimum number of board members. If you decide to have three initial board members, each person should agree to a different-length term, so members will not rotate at the same time.

#31. What qualities should I look for when choosing board members?

There are no firm criteria to apply to the initial board of directors. However, there are a few basic needs. A significant portion of your initial board is going to be decided for you, since it will generally be the people at the center of the organizing process.

In addition to the general responsibilities any new organization has to handle, board members must be willing and able to deal with the ever-present need to raise money. At the very least, they must show a willingness to learn how to raise money. Although a passion for the mission of the group is very important, the first question for an initial board member should always be, "How do we pay for it?"

Therefore, it is entirely appropriate to include individuals who have expressed a willingness to help financially. As the organizer, be prepared to have serious discussions with people who are in a position to be of financial assistance. Be honest about the needs of the organization as you understand them, and then seek the counsel of those who have offered to help. If you need to offer a board seat to an individual with networks in the philanthropic community, then do so.

Board members should not have their own agendas, nor should they use their positions on your initial board to advance their careers. This situation is not uncommon, particularly in cultural and artistic organizations where people whose qualifications make them suited for programming or operations instead seek board appointments. Sadly, they often realize too late that board responsibilities are much more difficult than they had envisioned. Such bad appointments are also hard to undo once the organization has incorporated and adopted formal bylaws.

#32. How should I choose the officers of the corporation?

Even if your initial board is no larger than the minimum suggested, select the officers of the corporation from the board. Anyone who assumes one of the leadership positions should be willing and able to carry out the responsibilities. Some states have articles of incorporation that request specific types of officers. There is no rule that prohibits offices from being shared, but it is not advisable.

The general duties of the officers of a nonprofit organization are similar to those of a for-profit corporation. It is a good idea for the initial board to adopt clear definitions of the officers' roles. You can refine the roles to suit your needs, and the responsibilities of each position should be spelled out in your bylaws so future boards and their officers can follow your guidance and your example.

#33. **What are the responsibilities of the president?**

The board president is responsible for much more than facilitating the meetings of the board of directors. They will become the public face of the organization, the contact person for every question anyone in the community may want to ask. They will also be the main advocate for everything your organization is trying to do, from attending early-morning business breakfasts to arranging lines of credit to overseeing programming issues to facilitating board and community meetings. It is common for the board president to be one of the organization's check signers. Although she won't manage the financial data, she should always have access to it.

As the organization grows and more people join at a decision-making level, either as staff or committee members, many of the initial board president's roles will diminish. In the beginning, however, the initial board president should be called upon to perform many tasks.

#34. **What are the responsibilities of the vice president?**

The official role of a vice president is to be available when the president is temporarily unable to fulfill his or her responsibilities or to be readily available as a permanent replacement should the president need to step down. On a volunteer board, the responsibilities go much further.

The vice president needs to be aware of everything that goes on in the organization, from knowing what the committees are working on to being familiar with the status of any programming.

The VP must be able to work in partnership with the president when needed. He or she also needs to be available on short notice to take on special projects such as chairing a committee.

#35. **What are the responsibilities of the secretary?**

The secretary needs to assume two independent roles. The internal role, often referred to as a recording secretary, involves generating and filing in a safe place all of the group's corporate documents, the minutes of meetings, mailing lists, and databases. The secretary takes accurate minutes during every board or public meeting and collects the minutes from the committee meetings. The secretary is also responsible for cleaning up rough meeting notes that will become part of the permanent record of the organization.

The second role is external and is often referred to as a correspondence secretary. That person's ongoing task is to handle all the official correspondence of the organization. These tasks have greatly expanded in the electronic age to include monitoring all e-mail traffic, keeping the organization's website current, and anything else that involves communication between the group and the broader community. The board member who assumes this role must be comfortable with e-mail and writing in general and will need to create reports within a regular time frame.

#36. **What are the responsibilities of the treasurer?**

First, this person should maintain the group's financial books, which involves basic checkbook balancing and bill paying. The treasurer is usually one of the official check signers and has access to any bank accounts or investments held by the group.

In consultation with the board president and the financial committee, the treasurer is responsible for preparing the yearly financial report for the IRS once the tax exemption (IRS Form 990) is obtained or for paying any federal corporate taxes if the tax exemption has not yet been received. The treasurer also makes sure that all local fees and taxes are paid.

The second role is to assist in developing the yearly operating budget. If projected budgets are necessary to qualify for funding opportunities or at the early stage for the application for nonprofit status, the treasurer should be directly involved in developing these documents for presentation to the full board and outside entities as necessary.

The third role for the treasurer, especially in the early stages of the organization's formation, is to oversee fundraising efforts. This role is not limited to making requests (though every board member needs to learn to do that). Rather, it is an opportunity to work on a long-term development strategy for sustainability.

The treasurer needs to be comfortable handling money and working with numbers. Although there are numerous software programs available to help with budget development and book-keeping, it is helpful to understand the basics.

#37. Should the members of the board of directors be paid?

The members of the initial board of directors must decide whether to pay themselves. That decision may be written into the bylaws if they so choose. The common assumption is that nonprofit boards are always voluntary. However, there is no law expressly prohibiting a nonprofit board from being paid, as long as that payment is considered "reasonable."

That said, your board is venturing into dangerous territory if its members choose to pay themselves. Not only will they run the risk of being liable for the excess benefit tax, they will also raise questions within the organization and the broader community about exactly how scarce funds are being spent.

About 5 percent of nonprofit organizations in the country compensate board members. If you decide as an organization to pay board members, seek legal advice from an attorney well versed in nonprofit law to avoid inadvertently crossing dangerous lines and placing your tax-exempt status in peril.

Your board may be reimbursed for reasonable expenses directly related to their activities as board members as long as there is a full and complete accounting for those costs. It is a good practice to submit estimates of the items well before the money is spent and to set limits on reimbursable expenses. These decisions can be handled through simple motions of the board at any regular meeting. Use the law and common sense as your guide.

#38.   What should be discussed at the first meeting of the board?

Unlike the first meeting of the organization, which can be an opportunity for brainstorming and general planning, the first meeting of the board of directors represents the beginning of your organization as a legal entity. It is also the time when your newly seated board needs to formally accept the documents necessary for incorporation, elect the officers, agree to move forward with the application for federal nonprofit status, open a bank account, and authorize a method for paying expenses.

The most important thing to keep in mind is that you are not only establishing an organization for the present, you are establishing a legal corporation that will survive past your personal involvement.

It becomes even more important that each document you helped write meets all of your needs as well as every need mandated by the group, the state, and the IRS, if you plan to pursue federal tax exemption.

#39. **What are the fiduciary responsibilities of the board?**

From a financial standpoint, it is the board's responsibility to keep the funds the group raises safe from risk. The board must make sure that all operational decisions are based on sound financial analysis. Maintaining the organization's financial integrity is the first thing associated with the word *fiduciary*, but the responsibility includes preserving the essence of the group for the present and the future.

As the organization matures and the committees, staff, and community volunteers come into their own, the board must temper risky options that may be presented. The board will need to weigh proposals that may not appear to be financial in nature but could potentially affect the group's finances if mistakes are made or if there is a lapse in attention.

Examine everything you consider doing in light of how it might affect the organization in the short term (attendance, positive media, etc.) and also how it might affect the group's financial well-being in the long term.

PART II

It's All in the Details

Chapter 5

INCORPORATION

#40. What are articles of incorporation?

Articles of incorporation tell the state and the general public about your organization. They say who you are and how you operate. If you plan to become a federally recognized nonprofit organization, articles of incorporation show that your organization complies with basic requirements. The articles also detail how the organization will be dissolved, if necessary, including the disposition of any remaining funds.

#41. How do I fill out my articles of incorporation?

Each state has its own requirements for the wording of articles of incorporation. Most states supply template articles containing their required language.

The first important section is the Name section (sometimes also identified as Article 1). Enter the name of your nonprofit exactly as you want it to appear on all subsequent legal documents. No one will edit or spell check what you put on the form. Any abbreviations or punctuation you use will remain as the name, so take this element seriously. Remember, if you use the word *the*, as in "The XYZ School for the Performing Arts," it stays. The same holds true for abbreviations in parentheses, often used for longer names. If you put it on the form as your name—again, identifying our example of a performing arts school as "XYZSPA"—it stays. Carefully read the instructions for requirements regarding words such as *Incorporated* and *Company*.

The next important section is the term of existence of your nonprofit. More often than not, this will be "perpetual," so check that box if it appears. This indicates you are planning to be in existence forever, as opposed to simply existing for one project. Of course, if you are incorporating for the purpose of a short-term project as a state nonprofit and have no plans to apply for federal tax exemption, indicate this on the form along with your projected date of dissolution.

For your address, post office addresses are fine for the organization and the initial board of directors, unless otherwise instructed. You will need to list an actual street address for the registered agent.

Some states require the North American Industry Classification System (NAICS), which was established by the Office of Management and Budget. Refer to the website *www.census.gov/eos/www/naics* to locate the NAICS classification that is closest to your nonprofit's mission.

#42.   How do I define the purpose of my nonprofit in order to meet IRS standards?

Defining your purpose in your articles of incorporation is much different than defining your purpose to your community and is incredibly important. When you are talking to the community, you will define your purpose in terms of the good you hope to do. The articles of incorporation follow a different set of rules.

The nonprofit corporation must adhere to the rules governing its financial transactions. Following these rules allows your organization to continue, and, in fact, succeed. For the IRS, you must define how you intend to operate from a financial standpoint. You must inform the IRS that you intend to follow both the letter and spirit of the regulations regarding nonprofit organizations. The IRS wants specific language.

To meet IRS requirements, use this *exact* language in your articles of incorporation: "The organization is organized exclusively for charitable, religious, educational, and scientific purposes under section 501(c)(3) of the Internal Revenue Code, or the corresponding section of any future federal tax code."

You may also want to add the following language to explain your purpose further: "Notwithstanding any other provision of these articles, this corporation shall not, except to an insubstantial degree, engage in any activities or exercise any powers not in furtherance of section 501(c)(3) purposes."

The IRS encourages applicants to go into additional detail to define their purpose more narrowly. Keep succinct any further language you choose to include.

#43.   How should I include the plans for dissolution of my nonprofit?

It may seem odd to plan how your organization will end just as you are preparing to begin, but the IRS requires every applicant for tax-exempt status to include in its articles of incorporation a clear plan for dissolution. Everyone involved must understand how money or other assets will be handled if or when the organization decides to stop functioning and elects to dissolve. This is to guarantee that any net earnings or assets held by a nonprofit organization will not benefit any individual or private shareholder.

There are two different ways to plan for this in your articles of incorporation. You can indicate that upon dissolution of your organization, you will distribute any remaining assets to another 501(c)(3) organization that will not be identified until your organization formally dissolves. This option can be tricky because it leaves a very important decision to people you may not know, who may choose to distribute funds in a way that is counter to the wishes of the current board. Further, if the organization does not formally dissolve but simply ceases operation, the last board may lose control of the remaining funds and a court will have to determine the final disposal.

The second option is to indicate that upon dissolution of your organization your funds will go to another organization that you name in your articles. The advantage here is that your organization can be certain that another nonprofit with a similar mission and overall approach will be the recipient of your assets and that the decision will be made when everyone is thinking clearly. You can include language to the effect that if that organization is no longer in existence or chooses not to accept the distribution, your board may then select another group.

#44.   **Can I amend the articles of incorporation once they're written?**

There may come a time when you want to make a change to your articles, and that's okay! It is entirely possible for an organization to change something in its articles of incorporation after they have been filed. In a perfect world, such changes would never be necessary, but fortunately everyone involved in the process realizes that mistakes happen and changes are required, so a smooth mechanism is available to amend your articles. Remember that because your organization is now a corporation recognized by the state and the articles are the legal basis for the corporation, any changes to those articles must be handled in a precise manner.

There are two separate parts to amending the articles of incorporation. First, your board must propose and pass the language, following the process spelled out in your bylaws to cover this exact situation. Second, you must file articles of amendment with the state secretary of state at the same address you filed the original incorporation documents. There is usually a small fee associated with the filing.

Do not make a habit of filing too many articles of amendment, but do use the option when necessary. Unlike your bylaws, which can be modified with little outside scrutiny, articles of amendment filed with your state become public record. Many groups hold off on changes as long as possible and then combine multiple amendments into one form to streamline the process.

#45.   Whom should I choose to be the registered agent for my organization?

The incorporation form in most states will have a line on which to identify your registered agent. This term also appears on forms provided by many local jurisdictions that require some kind of permit or license to conduct business in their area.

Once it is established, a corporation becomes a person in the eyes of the state. It has many of the rights and privileges of a real person, but it is obviously not a person who can be contacted or served with legal papers should the need arise. Therefore, a real person must agree to accept legal filings on behalf of the organization.

The person who becomes your registered agent can be anyone of your choosing. He or she can be a board member, anyone in your organization, or anyone in the larger community who is trusted by the organization and agrees to assume this role. It is not unusual for the registered agent to be identified in the bylaws as the current president of the board of directors or the executive director, with a mailing address readily available. As part of your annual reporting, note any changes in the person holding that position.

#46.   What is the difference between a registered agent and an incorporator?

While these roles can be handled by the same person, they are actually distinct. The role of registered agent continues as long as the organization exists. The person holding that role can obviously change over time, but the role remains.

The incorporator, on the other hand, prepares the articles of incorporation and delivers them to the state secretary of state. He or she agrees to be available by telephone or e-mail should questions come up. The incorporator might be your lawyer, a consultant you asked to assist with the process, or any member of your core group who agreed to manage the process. After the application has been approved and the certified copy with the stamp or seal of the secretary of state's office has been returned, the role of the incorporator is pretty much over—with your thanks!

#47.   How do I file the articles of incorporation?

State secretary of state offices usually handle nonprofit as well as for-profit corporate filings. Some states have authorized other offices to handle these documents. You can visit the National Association of Secretaries of State (NASS) website at *www.nass.org* for a list of office addresses. You will need to print out your articles of incorporation, sign them, and mail them to your state's office.

Provided everything has been properly filled out and you included the required fee, you will receive in response a formal document, which is embossed with the state seal, from the state government office that handles corporate filings. This certified document, which will be date stamped, is evidence of your incorporation status; be sure to make copies of it.

#48.   What address should I use for official nonprofit correspondence?

If you use an address that is not zoned for business use, the city may raise concerns about your venture. Government employees are bound by the law, and they must review your materials. All they will see is that you are a business and you have an office at a specific address.

Keep in mind that all local government employees have to go on are the forms you have submitted and any corresponding land-use code. If you find out that your office location is in a restricted area for any reason (usually involving zoning), ask the people in the office how to negotiate your way out of the problem. If your start-up office is someone's living room (a very normal circumstance), you may need to change addresses. If you have a building or are in the process of obtaining one, you may need to apply using a temporary address, pending your acquisition of necessary variances. This can be a long, complicated process, so seek professional advice from someone familiar with your situation.

#49.   How do I obtain a federal tax ID number?

You will need to obtain a federal tax number, also referred to as an Employer Identification Number (EIN), as soon as possible. This is the number the federal government and many state and local government agencies use rather than one person's social security number. Most of the government forms you fill out request this number, so you might as well get it now and check that task off your to-do list.

The fact that you do not have employees has no bearing on your need for an EIN. Most of these systems are set up with the expectation that while you may not need everything in the beginning, you will be set when the need arises.

Fortunately, obtaining a federal EIN is probably one of the easiest processes you'll go through while incorporating. There are three options:

1. Call 1-800-829-4933 to make your application. You'll have a federal tax number before you hang up.
2. Download IRS Form #SS-4 from *www.irs.gov*. Fill it out and mail it in.
3. Apply online. The confirmation letter will be mailed to you in about a week.

The person who applies for an EIN will need to use her personal social security number for reference. She will also need to have the organization's legal name and address with her. There is no liability incurred for using that social security number. The whole point of having the number is for standardized corporate record keeping.

#50.   **Do I need a state business license?**

All states require some form of license to conduct business. This is separate from the incorporation.

The articles of incorporation establish your organization as a separate and unique legal entity. The business license allows you to conduct business in the state. Generally speaking, you must first incorporate before you can obtain a business license, but verify the preferred order in your state. You'll also need to find out what registration numbers are required for each form. The articles of incorporation will remain on file with your secretary of state or corporations' office; the business license is handled through a department of licensing or department of revenue.

The purpose of the license is to facilitate your ability to collect taxes on behalf of the state and remit those taxes on an established schedule. The license will also enter your organization into the database for other state taxes, such as employment taxes, which you may be responsible for paying.

These taxes are unrelated to any federal tax exemption you may obtain. Your organization will be responsible for them whether or not you obtain tax exemption. State business licenses are generally valid for a specific time and then they must be renewed.

Do not allow your business license to lapse. It will jeopardize your ability to conduct business and leave you open for criticism in the community, which will negatively affect your ability to maintain your revenue stream.

#51. As a nonprofit, is my organization exempt from paying state income tax?

If you are operating in a state that has a tax on corporate income, ask as soon as possible about obtaining your exemption from that tax. More often than not, the state exemption will run in conjunction with the federal tax exemption, but you need to verify this with the office handling your state business license. In Montana, North Carolina, and Pennsylvania, you must make a separate application to your state to obtain a nonprofit tax exemption. Washington has a similar tax called a business and occupation (B&O) tax.

#52. Do I need a local business license?

It depends on where you are operating, but in general the answer is yes. A local business license, usually issued by your city and often referred to as a tax registration certificate, allows you to operate in your city. If your city or other local jurisdiction has its own sales tax system, this certificate will also be your authorization to collect those taxes on behalf of the local government and forward that money on an established schedule, much as you do for the state.

There is an annual cost associated with a local business license. As with other assorted fees, permits, and licenses, work it into your yearly budget as an operational expense.

The most difficult time for getting these licenses in place is during your start-up phase, when much of the work will fall to your treasurer. Once everything is established, these tasks will become a routine matter of staying current with your yearly obligations.

#53.   **Should I apply for a nonprofit mailing permit?**

As you plan to apply for federal tax exemption, consider applying for a nonprofit mailing permit to reduce your annual postal costs. Even with the increased use of e-mail, postage continues to be one of the major budget items in every nonprofit organization, particularly if you send out periodic solicitation letters. The United States Postal Service (USPS) has its own set of rules and criteria for authorizing organizations to mail at its reduced nonprofit rates.

The criteria for authorization are similar in many respects to the requirements to obtain your tax-exempt status, but there are differences. While a determination letter from the IRS is one of the documents necessary to establish your status for the USPS, it is not the only one. The application is available at *www.pe.usps.com/businessmail101/misc/nonprofitapplication.htm.*

Chapter 6

BYLAWS

#54. **What is the purpose of bylaws?**

Bylaws tell people within your organization how you conduct your internal business and how members relate to one another. The bylaws describe who makes up your membership and the responsibilities of everyone involved in the group, from the board and committees to staff and volunteers. Bylaws also outline the organization's commitment to fairness and nondiscrimination.

Within a generally accepted framework, your organization is free to decide how you will select future boards of directors, handle meetings, establish committees, hire staff, manage finances, and conduct business. As one of the earliest documents your organization will draft, bylaws are created before the stress of running an organization makes crafting a well-designed set more difficult.

The first few sections should cover housekeeping details. You need to state the formal name of the organization and the location where you conduct business. Once you cover the basics, it's time to detail the main parts of your organization's operation. Bylaws should make clear your mission to three groups: staff, volunteers, and the board of directors; your donors; and the IRS.

#55.   **How do I clearly convey the status of my organization as a charity?**

It's extremely important that you state in your purpose that you are a charity. The language must be clear so your future financial supporters understand exactly what you are planning to do.

You must establish positive relationships with these people in order to meet the IRS requirements to become and remain a public charity. Your supporters will want to be assured that your commitment to certain core principles that appear in your bylaws aligns with their values as well. The philanthropic community will often evaluate these basic elements well before any consideration is given to actual requests for financial support. The funding community will want to know that your organization understands the meaning behind the words *public charity.*

The IRS looks at an organization's bylaws to determine whether it is operating as a public charity. By definition, a public charity must receive a substantial part of its support in the form of contributions from publicly supported organizations, governmental units, and/or the general public. In addition, no more than one-third of support can come from investment income, and more than one-third of support must come from contributions, membership fees, and gross receipts from activities related to its exempt functions.

#56.   **How do I lay out the responsibilities of the board of directors?**

The first section or article in the bylaws is usually about the board of directors. This is a symbolic way of recognizing the importance of the board to the ongoing viability of a nonprofit organization.

The board must agree to carry out two primary tasks, each of which includes long lists of responsibilities.

First, the board must manage and oversee the board of directors, which includes its own meetings, meetings of any committees, elections, selection of officers, and other responsibilities.

Second, the board must maintain management or oversight of the organization, which includes fundraising or financial management, staffing, legal issues, real estate, and programming.

The board is responsible for calling and running its own meetings, which should be scheduled at regular intervals. All decisions that affect the organization are made at these meetings, and an accurate record (the minutes) should always be retained. The board is responsible for creating its committees and soliciting any outside advice it feels it needs to manage the organization.

Some boards find it advantageous to use an administrator to help manage the board's internal business. This selection is not a priority for the first stages of a start-up nonprofit; it is a decision that can be made later.

The board is also responsible for the group's financial management, and it is ultimately responsible for staffing, long-range planning, general policy decisions, and public perception. The board's fiduciary responsibilities will affect everything it does both within the organization and in the community. From both a legal and moral standpoint, how the board handles that responsibility will make or break the organization.

#57. How should I structure the membership options in my organization?

Laying out your membership structure is a major step in getting your organization off the ground. The type of membership structure you choose will say a great deal about how you plan to relate to the broader community, so examining a number of options makes sense. Each option carries its own set of advantages and disadvantages.

One possibility is restricting membership to the board. This is an entirely valid option, in which the board is also the entire voting membership. It nominates itself into office and then determines, by whatever agreed-upon means, how the organization will operate. Particularly in the formative stages, this option limits outside distractions from diverting the board while allowing it to remain focused on the immediate work that needs to be done.

Since this option excludes participation at the decision-making level by members of the community, it may lead to feelings of resentment among those who are not able to vote. This is not to suggest that the public cannot be involved in the organization. Once board decisions have been made, the board members may invite anyone they want to implement those decisions. However, those individuals, whether they are community volunteers or paid staff, are not voting members of the board.

The board is always free to invite guests to any meeting to participate in discussions and offer expertise. Likewise, members of the community who are active in the organization may ask to be invited. The only limitation is that only board members participate in decision-making.

You might also choose to open membership to the community. This opens the membership to people outside the board of directors, using clearly established criteria. Membership may require nothing more than active participation. There may be different membership levels, ranging from those who can vote to those who are simply on a mailing list.

The advantage of an open-membership system is that your organization will appear more inclusive and not prone to claims of cliquishness among the leadership. However, it opens your organization to political maneuvering by any determined group. This possibility can be mitigated by how board members are nominated, and the danger decreases as the organization matures, but it is something to keep in mind.

The third option is to combine elements of the other options so that you and the organization can be inclusive and still able to conduct the necessary work for your group. You can establish levels of membership that range from being on your mailing list to active membership that may involve voting rights.

Even if you choose not to have members, a mailing list of active people in the community, regardless of their legal membership status, will become a useful fundraising tool. Such a list is tangible evidence of the necessary community support your organization has established.

#58. How should I set up standing committees?

One of the most important functions of your bylaws is to identify the standing committees of the board and articulate their basic responsibilities. Membership on the committees is for the board to determine; at least one board member should be on every committee. Having only board members populate every committee is an option; in the beginning, it is normal for the committees to include only board members. In time, though, as you begin looking for individuals whose skills may be beneficial to your organization, consider opening up committee memberships. You may mandate in the bylaws exactly how the committees are to function, or you may leave that to the committee to determine. At a minimum, committees should establish regular meeting times and always record minutes of their discussions.

#59. What is the purpose of the finance/budget committee?

This committee exists to oversee financial affairs. It keeps these issues before the board and brings together the people best suited for the task of making the organization's finances run smoothly. The finance committee should maintain oversight of fundraising activities and of all actual and projected expenses. If these are not the people developing the working budget, they must have regular access to it.

#60. What is the purpose of the program committee?

The program committee is where the work of your organization is developed. This committee analyzes proposals from inside your organization or ones brought to you from the larger community for their suitability and appropriateness to your stated mission. The program committee may also become a portal into your organization for community members who want to take a larger role in the actual operations, making it an initial point of contact to your board.

Once the program committee evaluates projects, it may propose them to the full board for action. There can, of course, be countless variations in the process, which may involve staff, volunteers, and other constituencies, but the standing committees exist to spread out the actual work of running the organization and preparing action items for the board to consider.

#61. **What is the purpose of an advisory committee, and should my organization have one?**

Establishing an advisory committee is an excellent way to bring on board highly respected members of the community who support your mission but are too busy to commit to specific tasks. Advisory committee members are usually recruited through a personal invitation of a board member. They agree to be available to offer advice in their particular area of expertise, as well as open up their respective networks for periodic outreach and solicitations.

It is not too early, even in the formative stages, to begin thinking about whom you would approach to join the advisory committee. If you decide to approach someone you do not know, determine where your networks and that person's networks intersect and approach her from that point. Keep in mind that well-known people are frequently asked to lend their name and support to worthwhile organizations. Carefully plan how to present yourself and the group in order to give the best chance of creating a strong, respected advisory committee.

#62. **How can I use the bylaws to attract people to my organization?**

Your bylaws present a fine opportunity to let potential volunteers, potential funders, and general supporters know that you will be operating in a style and manner that meets your needs and theirs. This is particularly true as your organization enters into more detailed activities where funding sources may need to identify closely with the organization through its bylaws.

There is a fine line between creating bylaws that show how you plan to function internally so you can show external audiences that you are all on the same page and appearing to pander to a specific funding source. Remember all materials that have been developed since your founding will be examined, not simply one document. The best thing is to be honest and realistic.

Chapter 7

INTERNAL RECORDS AND BOOKKEEPING

#63.   What should be included in a meeting agenda and minutes?

Agendas and minutes are the basic records of your meetings. Keep the corrected minutes and make them available for future reference. Such referencing is essential if there is a question about who said what at a meeting or when you need the details of a particular vote.

An agenda is the list of topics to be covered at any meeting of the board—or of any committee of the board. The board may decide to adopt specific rules for putting items on an agenda. At this stage, however, follow a basic form and modify it when necessary.

Using standardized forms to establish your agenda, either as hard copy or as a template on your word processor, makes the task much easier and more streamlined.

The standardized form does not need to be elaborate. It should have a place for the date and the normal parts of the meeting as headers. Then fill in the template with specific details and include items such as:

- Special announcements and introduction of guests
- Approval of the minutes of the last meeting

- Changes or adjustments to the agenda
- Input from the audience or anyone other than board members
- Officer and/or staff reports
- Committee reports
- The date for the next meeting

Leave a space on your agenda template to insert, in minutes, how much time to devote to an agenda item. Select a timekeeper to watch the clock throughout the meeting and enforce the time limits agreed to in the agenda. This will move the meeting along and ensure that every topic is covered. Be sure that everyone agrees on the agenda before the meeting begins; encourage all board members to suggest additions or deletions, as well as times allotted for discussion.

Unlike the agenda, the minutes of the meetings of an incorporated nonprofit organization are legal documents. They are the record of how your public organization conducts its business. Although rare, there is the possibility that someone will ask to review the minutes, and you are obligated to permit him to do so. As with the agenda, many organizations design a basic form to make the task of recording the meeting a little easier on the secretary. Many groups often make an audio recording for their archives.

#64.   **What needs to be included in my nonprofit's financial records?**

Money can easily become an unnecessary source of strife for a fledgling nonprofit organization, which is why it's so important early on to establish a clear financial reporting system.

The IRS has specific requirements for what must be included in the annual financial report, Form 990. Because every organization operating with a federally recognized tax exemption must file this form, structure your bookkeeping from the beginning to make reporting easier. Although you may not need the details required in the form for every internal report, it is easier to delete something than to create required documents when you are busy with other tasks.

Regardless of who will ultimately be receiving your financial reports, make sure the basics are covered. Your main accounting must include the following:

- *A basic income/revenue statement*, with categories for salaries or consultant fees, office/postage expenses, and revenue specified in general terms
- *A balance sheet*, identifying particular categories such as accounts receivable and cash on hand
- *A statement of earmarked expenses*, in which your expenses are clearly allocated to program services (what you "do"), fundraising, operations, or the internal details of actually running the organization
- *A statement of expenses* broken out by the actual program service (i.e., educational mailings, a field trip, or a public lecture)
- *A support schedule* that describes your organization's sources of revenue (e.g., charitable donations, membership fees, investment income, etc.)

Although most reporting will not call for this level of detail, the IRS does, so it makes sense to design your entire financial environment to meet the most stringent requirements you will face. You can always skip unneeded details.

#65.   **What is Form 990-N?**

An organization holding a tax exemption from the federal government is relieved from paying any federal corporate income taxes but not from making annual reports detailing its financial situation. Such an organization must tell the federal government where its operating money came from and how it was spent. The completed form—Form 990—is considered a public document, open for examination by anyone at any time.

This transparency is one of the tradeoffs your organization must accept in exchange for nonprofit status—your organization is now public in every sense of the word. The IRS website, *www .irs.gov,* maintains a database open to the public. The site allows anyone to search for and read Form 990 or 990-N of any nonprofit in the country holding federal tax-exempt status (*www.irs.gov/ Charities-&-Non-Profits/Search-for-Forms-990-N-Filed-by-Small -Tax-Exempt-Organizations*).

Since most new nonprofits will have receipts in their first year well below the $25,000 threshold requiring them to file the complete Form 990, it is appropriate to include an explanation of Form 990-N here.

The process for filing is easy and straightforward. First, go to the IRS website, locate the Form 990-N link, and set up an e-Postcard account. Before you begin filling out the form, be sure you have the following necessary information at hand:

- Your Employer Identification Number
- Tax year (be careful not to insert the current calendar year)
- Legal name and mailing address of the organization
- Name and address of the principal officer (the name of your board president is sufficient)
- Any other names the organization uses (this enables cross-referencing by people conducting searches)
- Website address, if you have one
- Confirmation that annual gross receipts are normally $25,000 or less
- A statement that the organization has terminated or is terminating (going out of business), if applicable

Organizations with gross receipts over $25,000 must file the complete Form 990. If you followed the basic guideline in setting up your books in line with the needs of that form, filling out the form and filing it should not present any trouble.

#66.   How will the recent changes to the 990-N affect my nonprofit?

If your organization is filing the full Form 990, you need to be aware of a number of significant changes that have been made to the form and the level of detail required. Specifically, Part VI seeks information regarding the board of directors, and their family and/or business relationships to one another. If your organization is new and small enough not to be required to submit the longer Form 990, these requirements will not immediately affect you. However, these requirements will affect you in the future as your organization grows.

The new requirements seek detailed information about your board of directors, such as:

- Whether they or any of their family members engaged in any business transactions with the organization
- Whether entities (of which they or their families owned more than 35 percent) engaged in any business transactions with the organization
- Whether they do business, other than as a member of the general public, with another board member, officer, or key employee, or with an entity of which another board member, officer, or key employee is a director, officer, or owner of more than 35 percent
- Whether they have a family relationship with any other director, officer, or key employee of the organization
- Whether they are a director, officer, or owner of greater than 10 percent of an entity of which another of the organization's directors, officers, or key employees is a director, officer, or owner of greater than 10 percent

#67. **What types of projected revenue sources should I include in my projected budget?**

When you are developing your initial budget, few things are more difficult than identifying revenue sources. Everyone around you will find ways to spend money; to develop a budget, however, you must identify sources to raise funds. Most nonprofit organizations start out with barely enough money to rent a room in which to meet, so the idea of looking beyond the immediate to attaining viability can be a challenge.

Hopefully you've already been evaluating your community and making contacts. Now is the time to use those fledgling relationships. The local business community, the media outlets, and the people you see every day may become your future individual or corporate sponsors, and you should include them in your budget.

Evaluate your membership options. If members pay dues, enter this money as both current and projected income. As you identify appropriate grants, include those sources as possible or projected income. Do not include these sources if the grant is something you have no chance of securing. This is not a time to live in a fantasy.

If you will be receiving a fee for services and are able to provide an estimate of the projected income from those fees, that is an income source; include it in your projected budget. The sales of any product that complies with the strict requirements regarding "unrelated business income" are also eligible for inclusion as projected income. Consult a professional tax advisor who is familiar with your situation before including any sales in your projected income.

#68. **Can my nonprofit engage in unrelated business activity?**

A nonprofit organization can, under limited circumstances, engage in commercial activity, provided it pays the Unrelated Business Income (UBI) tax. If your organization is considering this type of activity or planning to solicit or accept sponsorships, it is wise to consult a tax lawyer to make certain your plans line up with current law.

There are three main criteria used to determine if your activities are UBI:

1. Would the activity generally be considered a trade or business?
2. Is the activity a regular, repeated occurrence as opposed to a one-time special situation?
3. Is the activity not substantially related to your organization's exempt purpose?

If you answered yes to any of these questions, the income source you may be considering may well be unrelated business income for which you will need to file a Form 990-T—and yes, the T stands for tax (*www.irs.gov/pub/irs-pdf/f990t.pdf*). You then will be obligated to pay the tax due.

Many organizations are using the Internet as an outreach tool and as a way to market goods and services. If your organization chooses to do this, it is important that any items you offer on your website are clearly aligned with the mission of the group and do not enter the gray area of UBI.

#69. **What are capital expenses, and how do they fit into the projected budget?**

A capital expense is money you plan to spend on things that are going to last longer than one year, are often fairly expensive, and are necessary for the functioning of your organization. Such expenses might include the purchase of computers, a vehicle, or even a building.

Capital expenses will require a unique line or a complete section in your start-up budget; you must keep those expenses separate from your other operating costs since they will mostly be one-time expenses and because it may be possible to spread the expense out over several years' balance sheets.

Before you can figure out what you will need in the future and what dollar amount to attach to those needs, take stock of what you currently have. Capital expenses will be different for every organization, and to some extent, they are program-specific.

A direct benefit of the ongoing self-assessments undertaken by the board members is the ability to identify what they believe would help the organization fulfill its mission. Some of those needs will involve capital expenses spread out over many years, which will also form the beginning of these line items in your budget.

Office equipment is a very common capital expense. For budget purposes, keep equipment (e.g., computers, copiers, etc.) separate from the office supplies (e.g., paper and pens, etc.), because the equipment will outlast the supplies.

The reasons to keep large capital expenses separate are numerous:

1. The costs involved may overshadow your general operating expenses, making it appear you are already in the red without having done a thing.
2. It is likely the actual payments for these items will be prorated over many months, if not years. You must be able to show that clearly in your budget, especially if you are projecting the budget out three, five, or seven years.
3. It will be to your advantage to point directly to capital expenses when discussing your funding needs with potential supporters. Many individuals and philanthropic organizations are restricted from directly supporting operations. Helping to offset capital expenses is permitted because it is considered a long-term investment in your organization.

#70.   **What is depreciation?**

No discussion of capital expenses would be complete without an understanding of depreciation. Factoring depreciation into your projected budget allows for accurate forecasting.

Depreciation is a means of measuring the amount of monetary value something loses from the time your organization purchases it to a set time in your fiscal year. You will use formulas to determine the value of depreciation of anything of value you report on your Form 990, so having these values in your current and projected budget is a good idea.

#71.   **How should I calculate depreciation for my budget?**

Generally, depreciation is calculated by dividing the cost of the asset by its useful life. If a $100,000 piece of equipment, also called an asset, has a useful life of ten years, then you calculate depreciation by dividing $100,000 by 10 to get $10,000 per year.

Each year the organization must show that $10,000 as an expense of doing business, and these numbers need to appear in your projected budget. You'll enter these calculations on Form 990, which you will complete each year. Adding the total amount of depreciation registered by all active assets gives your organization's total depreciation expense for that year.

Depreciation numbers will give any prospective funder an accurate—if sometimes unflattering—snapshot of your real financial health.

If your accounting shows you are unable to replace worn-out equipment and are postponing the purchase of needed big-ticket items, it means you need to step up your fundraising efforts. On the good side, if you are just starting out and the organization's main assets consist of secondhand office equipment and furniture from the local thrift shop, the depreciation number will be very low and will look good in comparison to a group that owns a lot of things but is not able to upgrade regularly.

#72. **Should I include projected staffing expenses in my budget?**

When a nonprofit organization is first formed, everyone may be willing to volunteer their time and expertise because they believe strongly in the mission. However, as you develop your budget, you should begin contemplating eventual staffing needs. It may be a year or two before you can compensate personnel, but having a line in your budget to accommodate that possibility will place your group well ahead of the game. Start by looking at the board's assessment of where the organization should be in the next few years and pick out instances where it is clear the group may need an "outside" person to assist. The first couple of years you may need only a compensated consultant to help with a board retreat or an accountant to review your books or prepare your Form 990.

One of the common misunderstandings about nonprofits is the notion that no one should be paid. Nothing is further from the truth, but there are a few basic rules that must be clearly reflected in both the current and projected budget.

First, anyone employed or contracted must do so at an agreed-upon fee for his or her services. A sliding-scale fee is not acceptable or legal, since it would allow that person to benefit personally from the organization.

If it appears that someone is receiving a fee well above the community standards for a similar position, the organization runs the risk of being penalized for an excess benefit transaction. These fees must be reported on Form 990 and will be carefully scrutinized by the IRS. Excess benefit transactions can lead to increasingly severe penalties, up to and including a revocation of your tax-exempt status.

#73.   How do I include in-kind labor in my budget?

The time and expertise of your volunteers have real monetary value that your budget should reflect. Although no money is changing hands, work is being done. If the people doing that work charged the organization market fees, it would represent a substantial sum.

It is therefore appropriate to assign a monetary value to the tasks and determine the fair value of the donated labor needed. You can find out the real rate by calling a few people who do that work for a living.

#74.   What is an "ideal" budget breakdown for a nonprofit organization?

As you begin to factor in budget items related to administration, it is good to strive for an 80–10–10 goal:

- 80 percent of your expenses to your charitable purpose
- 10 percent of your expenses to administration
- 10 percent of your expenses to fundraising

Of course, these are guidelines based on best-case scenarios, but they give you a baseline. Investment funds kept in savings accounts are not part of these percentages. That money is carried on the books as investments. The only administrative expense associated with savings accounts might be a transaction, but otherwise nothing of any consequence.

#75.   How many "authorized check signers" should my organization have?

Although there are no hard rules in this area, common practice suggests it is best to limit the check signers to the board president, the board treasurer, and one other person. That individual may be a trusted volunteer or the lead person required to draw funds in the course of a major project.

The third check signer can rotate as necessary, and there may be extended periods when no one has that position. When the organization grows enough to have an operations manager or director, that person will customarily become a check signer to facilitate his responsibilities.

#76. Is it okay to keep some pre-signed checks in the office?

No one will officially recommend keeping a small number of pre-signed checks, but it is a common practice, especially in small organizations run by volunteers, to have a few checks that already have one signature and only need the second signature to make the check legal.

If your account requires only one signature, then you are able to use a check immediately. It isn't possible to predict when an emergency will arise that requires immediate access to the checking account. If one signer is out of town or otherwise unavailable, having that check kept in a safe location known to very few people will make all the difference.

#77. What is a commercial bank?

When you are starting out as a new nonprofit, it is imperative to find a bank that will best suit your needs. Keep in mind that as banking laws change, so too will the services offered by a particular bank.

A commercial bank works with businesses. Businesses have unique needs; for example, some businesses need a commercial bank that can accommodate a large volume of credit card payments and cash deposits. Commercial banks also often function as retail banks, serving individuals along with businesses, and usually provide basic services such as savings and checking accounts, loans for real and capital purchases, lines of credit, letters of credit, payment and transaction processing, and foreign exchange.

#78.   What is a retail bank?

A retail bank works with consumers, otherwise known as retail customers, providing basic banking services to the general public, including checking and savings accounts; certificates of deposit (CDs); safe deposit boxes; mortgages; auto, boat, and miscellaneous home improvement loans; and unsecured and revolving loans such as credit cards. You probably use a retail bank for your personal checking account. In addition to helping consumers, retail banks also serve businesses, so they, too, can function as commercial banks.

#79.   What is a credit union?

Credit unions are nonprofit organizations owned by the "members" or customers; they traditionally strive for service over profitability. These organizations have the same types of personnel as banks. Upper management consists of a board of directors that makes decisions about credit union operations. This board is composed of elected volunteers who are also credit union members who want a say in the operation of the business.

Credit unions are required to limit their membership to people who have a common bond. This bond may be geographic, religious, or occupational, but it must exist or the entity risks losing its status as a credit union.

Credit unions typically offer the same products and services as larger banks. However, some choose not to offer every product and service, because they do not do the same volume of business as larger banks. Banks can afford to have products that get customers in the door but do not bring in much money themselves. Credit unions are more likely to offer only the products and services used by a large portion of the membership.

Deposits are insured very much like bank deposits, but the two types of institutions are insured by different organizations. The National Credit Union Share Insurance Fund (NCUSIF), financed by the credit unions and not the federal government, handles all deposit insurance for a credit union. It offers the same level of protection as the more familiar Federal Deposit Insurance Corporation (FDIC), financed by the federal government.

#80. **What are savings and loan associations?**

Savings and loan associations (S&Ls) are for-profit corporations with investors who hope to realize a profit on those investments. They're primarily involved in real estate, making mortgage loans and accepting savings deposits. S&Ls handle most traditional banking needs, including business transactions.

#81. **What is a deposit-only account?**

Deposit-only accounts are an excellent way for the public to contribute to your organization. Your bank or credit union will set up an account, usually with an easily remembered name, and anyone at any time may make a deposit. The contributor will have a record of the deposit for his or her records, and the deposit will go directly into your organization's auxiliary account or into your working account.

#82. **What is a certificate of deposit?**

Certificates of deposit (CDs) are debt instruments issued by banks and other financial institutions to encourage individual or organizational investors to put money in their bank. The investor receives a set rate of interest in exchange for lending the bank or credit union money for a predetermined length of time. Maturities on certificates of deposit can range from a few weeks to several years. The interest rate your organization earns increases in proportion to the amount of time the money is in the CD.

One of the advantages of a CD is that your organization can calculate the earnings you can expect at the outset when you take out the CD. Certificates of deposit are fully insured by the FDIC and earn slightly more interest than a basic savings or checking account. This makes CDs an easy, safe way to save money in the long term.

However, there is a tradeoff. To earn the highest interest rates, you must opt for longer maturity, which means you lose access to the funds or must pay a substantial penalty if you cash them out early.

#83.   What is a money market?

Money markets offer many of the same benefits as CDs with the added features of a checking account. Technically speaking, a money market is more or less a mutual fund that attempts to keep its share price at a constant level of $1. Professional money managers will take the funds you deposit in the money market and invest them in minimal risk instruments such as Treasury bills, savings bonds, and CDs. Your organization will receive payments from the interest the money market earns.

Investors can open a money market account at most financial institutions. Generally, funds are accessed with checks. Depositing money in a money market is as easy as depositing cash into a savings or checking account. Cash is immediately available for other investments or other needs.

On the downside, some financial institutions limit the number of checks that can be drawn against the account in any given month. The rate of interest is also directly proportional to the investor's level of deposited assets—not to maturity, as is the case with CDs.

#84.   **Should I invite bank representatives to my nonprofit's events?**

The days of the town banker who knows everyone and is always willing to lend a hand or offer advice are generally gone. However, it is important to establish solid working relationships with people in your local bank or credit union who specialize in nonprofit businesses.

You'll value the relationship you have with these bankers when you need their assistance to secure a loan or establish a line of credit to improve some part of your operations. Many newer nonprofits do not have the financial track record needed for a conventional loan, so they need to know someone in the institution who is familiar with alternative programs and knows how to navigate the system.

Your financial paperwork will give the people in your bank or credit union most of the information they need. If you are applying for a loan, perhaps for construction or to remodel an existing facility, most of the review process is impersonal.

However, inviting bank employees to visit your site or attend one of your programs will help make them aware of who you are, what you are doing, and why you are doing it. Invite them into your organization as members of the community, not just as bankers. They may be able to refer you to someone in the community who is interested in your mission and may be able to help repair a leaky roof or upgrade your office equipment.

These visits will give everyone involved in the management of your organization an opportunity to chat informally and learn about one another. A personal connection can accomplish far more than a paper application. With an established relationship, the possibilities for increased cooperation will also grow.

As your business plan evolves or as you consider major capital expenses, stay in touch with the nonprofit specialists in your bank. They will have valid ideas and suggestions that you may never have considered. They represent a terrific resource, so use them.

#85.   **How do I establish my nonprofit's financial credibility?**

Unfortunately, there is no simple trick for an organization to establish its financial credibility. Regardless of how you and your organization choose to manage your funds, it is going to be a constant, unrelenting struggle. The sooner you recognize that fact, the sooner you can make plans.

When many people hear the term *startup*, they wince, thinking immediately of some harebrained scheme that has no chance of success. Some people also have a negative opinion about the term *nonprofit organization*, so startup nonprofit organizations often find it difficult to establish themselves as credible entities. However, there are practices and programs you can adopt at the very beginning that will assist in the process.

First, meeting all your financial obligations, major or minor, is essential to establishing and maintaining your overall credibility in the community. Much of this responsibility falls to your treasurer or that person's designee. They must ensure checks are in the mail on time and no late fees or overdrafts appear on your bank statements.

When you have good financial news, spread the word. You are going to get your financial footing in due course, and those grant applications are going to bring the results you desire. When they do, it is both natural and perfectly acceptable (unless you've specifically been requested to keep quiet) to tell your membership, the broader community, and especially other grant-makers.

As soon as you receive funds in a competitive cycle, you are going to find increased interest from other funders. The hardest task is securing that first award.

PART **III**

Moving Forward

Chapter 8

FUNDRAISING

#86. How should I involve my nonprofit's committees in fundraising?

A standing responsibility of every committee established in your bylaws should be to assist in securing funding for any project or other expense item it recommends for the organization. This is especially applicable to programming, building, or similar committees that will be researching and proposing ways the organization can fulfill its mission, usually involving the appropriation of funds.

Require your committees to suggest ways to offset the expenses involved in their proposals. This task will help spread the overall fundraising responsibility and provide a true sense of ownership for active committee members. Not only are they going to be proposing action items to the board, but they will also be offering concrete suggestions on how to pay for their proposals.

#87. How should I involve community volunteers in fundraising?

In the early stage of your organization, everyone will need to share some of the responsibility for fundraising. The general orientation given to all new volunteers should include an overview of the finances that allow your organization to function.

They don't need to read and evaluate the projected five-year budget, but they do need to be aware that the organization, while it is a nonprofit, is not isolated from the many challenges in the general economy. All outreach material—newsletters, websites, everything that is designed for general distribution to your volunteers—should include a way for people to contribute, either by pledges or by making a donation on the spot. Your fundraising must become as much a part of your organization as everything else you do.

#88.   What level of financial support should I expect from board members?

Among the first questions you will face from any potential funder will be the level of direct financial support you've already secured from your board of directors. It is an appropriate question, so do not be offended. It is normal for any individual or representative of other organizations to want to know that before you seek funds to carry on your mission, you have fully exhausted every area of support in your immediate circle.

Never be ashamed about asking for money to carry out your mission. There is an entire cottage industry of people who make these requests as well as those who consult with groups to develop comprehensive fundraising campaigns and ultimately make the requests themselves.

You'll need to decide upon the actual percentage of the annual operating budget you are going to seek directly from the board (which, by extension, includes family members). Prepare to make this figure known to other funders when they ask. Many organizations require a minimum level of financial support of all sitting board members as a direct means of maintaining their involvement.

The amount of the yearly contribution does not need to be excessive, and it should reflect the actual abilities of the board members to secure funds. However, make it known that you are serious about the need to raise money and are willing to lead by example.

#89.   Should board members be able to fulfill their financial obligations through in-kind contributions?

If you decide to establish a policy requiring prospective and current board members to be responsible for fundraising during the period they serve on the board, consider making periodic in-kind contributions an option to meet that commitment. There are very likely things of value the organization needs, which an in-kind or other noncash donation of approximate value would satisfy. Board members could donate office space, legal services, income-producing rental property, and other services.

#90.   How can I elicit donations from my existing contacts?

Your existing contacts form the base, the core, of all subsequent fundraising activities. Now you must establish a database to track your existing contacts, as well as future contacts who will become your donor base. As simple as it may sound, the only way people will know you need money is if you tell them.

A good fundraising incentive to use is the promise of special perks for donors. Update contacts in your database about everything you are doing so they feel part of the exciting adventure. Consider offering special meetings or tours limited to your donors and supporters. Tours and one-on-one lunches with board members or coordinators are a great way to thank these people for their support and provide the personal attention that is essential to maintaining long-term relationships.

Your organization needs to become as much a part of the families of your supporters as their kids and pets. If you plan to send out holiday notices or solicitations, make it a priority to do so on time. If you intend to have members-only receptions during the year, budget those activities into your yearly plans.

#91.   How do I establish a history for my organization?

Maintain careful, complete, and accurate records of everything you do, including your meetings and financial transactions, any media coverage, and your public relations material. This level of record-keeping is necessary to meet legal requirements and to establish a paper trail. A paper trail is a verifiable history of your organization for presentation to potential funders.

If your organization is so new that the history is too short to present with any degree of confidence, adjust your narrative slightly to explore the history of the individuals who started the organization and tell their stories. Explain how they came together to form this new organization. Press clippings of their activities will provide the needed tangible record of who you are even if the articles don't discuss the organization itself.

Consider keeping a scrapbook. The book can be a simple loose-leaf binder filled with material about your founders, your board, and your current activities. It will bring everything into perspective.

#92.   What is the common grant application?

Many regions of the country have a version of a common grant application, which grantmakers and grantseekers agree to use. Your local grant writing association, discussed in Question #93, will have information particular to your area. The national listing and general information is available on the web at *www.common grantapplication.com*.

#93.   What is a grant writing association?

Many areas of the country have associations for grant writers to meet one another, network, and further enhance their profession. These organizations can be located through an Internet search. Consider having anyone directly involved in your development activities join these groups.

Every grant-writing association functions differently, but they hold regular meetings, often luncheons or something similar, where regional grantmakers are invited to share their expertise and perspectives to help their counterparts, the grant writers, work more effectively. Approach these organizations when your organization is starting up; after all, everyone in the room was, at some point, where you are now.

#94.   How much money should we raise from public versus private funding sources?

As your board and consultants develop a fundraising plan, break down how you would like to spend the money (operations, capital development, staffing, programming, etc.) and where you intend to raise it. You have two choices: public financing or private financing. The IRS has already helped you by mandating that a minimum amount—one third—of your total income must come from public sources.

Show hard numbers representing these percentages in the preliminary budget you provide as part of your application for tax exemption and then stick to it in the future. The IRS monitors a new 501(c)(3) organization for five years to make certain it is indeed operating as a public charity and is securing at least the minimum percentage of its operating budget from public sources.

On a basic level, public funding can be broken down as:

- Government funding
- Funding from other public charities
- Other

#95.   **What is government funding?**

Government funding can come from any level of government, from federal to state or city. It can include everything from arts commissions and education departments to public service agencies and municipal humane societies. If the entity receives funds from taxes and has as part of its purpose the requirement to fund activities of nonprofit organizations, it falls under this umbrella. To learn what government grants are available is a tremendous task; begin by researching agencies with a connection to your particular mission.

Tap into the many listservs and newsletters maintained by the agencies and departments you work with to understand their funding cycles and application deadlines and to get a general feel for what may be available to you as a new nonprofit.

#96.   **What is foundation funding?**

Securing funds from other charities is considered public funding when it involves another nonprofit organization whose purpose is to contribute funds to organizations such as yours.

Since the funding organization is operating as a tax-exempt charity and also raised its money, for the purpose of this discussion its funds to you are considered public.

Other public funding might include members of the general public acting as individual contributors, income derived from membership fees, or gross receipts for services directly related to the mission or the tax-exempt function. Box-office revenue from public events sponsored by an exempt arts organization is another example of public funding.

#97.   **What is private funding?**

Private funding comes primarily from corporate entities and private endowments, particularly at the start-up phase. In return, these contributors will receive good publicity and that ever-important tax deduction. Corporate support often takes the form of advertising (either at your events or in publications), which brings the donor valuable publicity and helps your organization secure much-needed funds.

Many larger corporations have a charitable arm, often identified as a foundation, whose purpose is to assist nonprofits in their service area or in the community where the corporation's employees live. Identify those corporate-sponsored foundations and begin to develop the relationships you will need when their application cycle comes around.

#98. How should I structure a comprehensive fundraising campaign?

Many organizations manage to survive for a long time without a clear fundraising plan, relying solely on random solicitations of friends and supporters for funds. Eventually, however, most realize they need to develop a focused, four-part plan, designed for a month or a year, to give a sense of stability to operations and enhance their overall ability to carry out their mission. Those four parts are:

1. How much money you intend to raise
2. Why you need that money
3. How you intend to raise it
4. A timeline

#99. What should be the goal of my fundraising campaign?

The goal may be directly related to increasing operational capacity, or general outreach, or to increase membership. It may aim to hire a staff person or many staff people, or it may be to repair a wall, fix the plumbing, or put on a new roof. Whatever the case, the goal needs to be the amount of money you, as an organization, intend to raise.

If you recently completed the IRS Form 1023 to apply for your nonprofit determination, the projected budget you included in that application will be a good place to start. Be realistic. Looking at your cash on hand and then looking at the amounts you intend to spend over the next few years will give you the difference—or the amount you need to raise.

#100.   How should my campaign discuss our intention for the money?

Once an amount or goal is determined, you need to explain in detail why you need that money. Do not assume your audience will already be familiar with your organization, or that they have read all your assorted publications or meeting minutes. You need to educate the reader about your budget, how the amount/goal fits into that budget, exactly how it will be spent, and the consequences if the goal is not met (if you need to cease, limit, or not expand services).

#101.   How should my campaign discuss our plan for getting things done?

Identifying how much money you need and how you intend to spend it is the easy part. Now you need to articulate how you plan to raise it. This is also where you present the details of what activities you are able to take on and what totals you expect to bring in from those activities.

Estimate what it will cost to carry out the plan by creating a budget specifically for all the fundraising activities you plan to carry out. There are many ways to raise money! The determining factor is the number of volunteers or compensated staff available to do all the planning and execute the activities.

#102.   What is the difference between a fundraising plan and a fundraising campaign?

A fundraising plan is your organization's general plan for how to raise money in the long term. A campaign, on the other hand, focuses on a more specific goal for which your organization is trying to raise money, and might be held to a more restrictive timeline.

#103.   How do I develop a timeline?

The urgency of the project will also help determine the timeline. If you live in a rainy climate and the roof leaks, you need the money to fix the roof, and you need it as quickly as possible. Conversely, if you are operating a music club and want to rotate the local artwork, or perhaps you are running a garden society and would like to re-design your newsletter, you can plan on a longer campaign. Even with a clearly understood budget, well-articulated needs, and an excellent explanation of how you plan to carry everything through, projects will not get done if you don't establish a timeline.

#104.   How can I use house parties for fundraising?

House parties have become very popular in the last few years, in large part due to the relative ease of organizing them, low over-head, and good financial returns. Selected individuals who share a common interest are invited to the parties held in private homes.

The program can be simple, but it should include a table with informative literature, a short video presentation, and a brief talk by your board president or another highly respected person whom the attendees know. Follow the program with a formal request for contributions. You can keep overhead costs very low with donated food and drink.

#105.   How can I use auctions for fundraising?

Benefit auctions have been catching on as a means for organizations to make a considerable amount of money. There is a lot of pre-event work associated with this option. You must verify with your tax advisor how to navigate local or state regulations pertaining to benefit auctions and be prepared to document the entire event to remain compliant with the IRS. Remember, you may be incurring a tax liability and not all funds may be deductible, so do not hold an auction without doing your homework. There are numerous software applications available to assist nonprofit organizations with the bookkeeping associated with benefit auctions. Check out *www.readysetauction.com.*

#106.   How can I use benefit concerts for fundraising?

It's likely that benefit concerts will come up in fundraising discussions at some point. Unless you are working with A-list talent who are donating their fees and all ticket sales, concerts are terrific for outreach but are rarely a surefire way to raise funds. If you are determined to hold one, contract with a professional promoter in your region who knows the business. Negotiate a fee and then let that person take the project to its conclusion.

#107.   How can I use phone banks for fundraising?

Receiving phone call solicitations is annoying, but organizations that use phone banks find them very effective. There are a number of large national phone bank operators who work exclusively with nonprofits and are worth investigating.

#108. How do I use direct deposit systems for fundraising?

Internet programs like PayPal allow people to donate directly into your organization's bank account via a link or button on your website. In addition to simply accepting donations through any of the direct deposit systems, consider using them for event ticket sales or to accept payments for books or recordings you may offer. These systems can also be used as a virtual reception area/gift shop for visitors interested in learning more about your organization.

#109. How do I use Kickstarter for fundraising?

In recent years, one development in online fundraising that's been getting considerable attention is crowdsourcing. Kickstarter.com is one of the most prominent crowdsourcing sites, focusing mainly on creative projects that need funding. Your organization provides a fundraising goal and deadline, as well as a detailed description of the project you are trying to fund. Many organizations choose to offer rewards, such as T-shirts or mugs, for different levels of donations. Donors give money through the site, rather than directly to the organization, and the organization receives the money only if they meet their fundraising goal by their stated deadline, so be realistic when crafting your goal and timeline. If the goal is not met, the money is returned to the donors.

#110. How do I use Indiegogo for fundraising?

Indiegogo.com is another crowdsourcing website, which operates in a similar manner to Kickstarter, but is more inclusive of non-creative goals and organizations from outside the United States. It differs in one respect: It offers a funding model that is not all-or-nothing like Kickstarter. Instead, fundraisers are given the option to choose between the all-or-nothing model or a more flexible model in which fundraisers are allowed to keep what they earn, even if they don't reach their stated goal.

#111. How do I use DonorsChoose for fundraising?

DonorsChoose.org is a crowdsourcing website that deals with education needs of K–12 schools only. If your organization is education related, it may be worth looking into fundraising on this site rather than one of the more general options.

#112. How many online services should my website provide?

Online ticket sales and the ability to offer/provide services or conduct fundraising auctions online have completely revolutionized the ability of nonprofit groups to generate income. Investigate your options for providing as many services online as is practical. Just make sure that all the items you list online are within your mission statement and are not subject to the UBI tax.

#113. How does online fundraising save money?

As a practical matter, no longer having to print paper copies of everything will result in substantial and immediate cash savings. In addition, you'll save money by no longer having to store and insure auction items or books or other items you sell through your website.

#114. How do I provide a complete online shopping experience?

In order to provide a more complete shopping experience your website will require extensive modifications to accommodate a shopping cart and all the options that accompany it. You may need to open a special "merchant account" with your bank to enable credit card purchases made through your site to be directly deposited into that account. The costs associated with setting up that system will be recouped quickly, because your audience of potential supporters is now worldwide.

#115. What are some examples of in-kind contributions?

In-kind contributions are types of donations that are not financial; instead, they are donated time or services that have monetary value. Some examples are a professional athletic trainer donating a few hours a week to run a health class or a local print shop donating printing for your auction catalog. Each of these services has real value. However, since no cash changes hands, the contributions are considered in-kind.

#116. Are in-kind contributions tax deductible?

Your organization can and should attach a monetary value to the contribution and include that amount in your budget on the in-kind line in your income section. Determine the current fair-market value of goods or services and use those figures in your budget. For determining salary amounts, use the current salaries the exact service would cost if you had to contract an outside source.

Most people make in-kind contributions because of their interest in your cause. However, once a dollar amount is attached to that contribution for the purposes of your organization's accounting, that amount may be deductible from the contributor's federal income tax.

Chapter 9

BOARD DEVELOPMENT AND STAFFING

#117. What is board development?

Board development is a fancy term to describe the need to keep a volunteer board of directors engaged and excited about their organization
and everything taking place within it. In an ongoing, practical sense,
board development is also a reminder to remain constantly alert for
new potential board members. Current members will choose to step
aside or not seek re-election, and it will be necessary to replace them.
Additionally, shifting needs and expanding membership may create
new seats that need to be filled by individuals with specific talents.

#118. How should the bylaws influence board development?

You determined the mechanics of how to add new people to your
board when you drafted your bylaws. As you think about the deliberate process of creating a board of directors, circulate copies of
those bylaws to everyone, even the current board who may have
drafted them. It's a good idea to refresh everyone's memory about
the agreed-upon process.

#119. How should fundraising play into board development?

It's natural to assume that the ability to fundraise should play a large part in board development, but that is not necessarily the case. Although fundraising will remain an important responsibility for any member of a nonprofit board, taking a holistic approach to board development by incorporating governance, outreach, and long-range goals into your thinking will make your organization much healthier in the long term.

#120. Should I engage a consultant for board development?

Yes. They may have limited direct knowledge of the personalities and dynamics of your particular organization, but they will have an expert understanding of how small groups function and will be able to help your board reach its full potential.

Many nonprofit boards are made up of people who have a passion for the organization's mission rather than an acute business sense. As a result, there is an industry of consultants who use a combination of education and experience to fill the holes in nonprofits on a temporary basis. If you find your organization in a situation where professional consulting is necessary, it is a sure sign that the nonprofit is maturing and is able to recognize its needs before problems occur.

#121. How do I activate the nominating committee?

If your bylaws require the establishment of a formal nominating committee to facilitate the search for new board members, you can start the process with a simple agreement of the board by recorded motion to establish and activate such a committee. The nominating committee should work closely with the board and any outside consultant to establish the board's needs and determine how best to fill those needs by inviting individuals from the community into your organization as potential board members.

#122.   **Should committee membership be a route to the board?**

The committees established through language in the bylaws will eventually become far more than a way of distributing the work to fulfill your mission. They can evolve into a training ground for potential board members who are already accustomed to the way the organization functions. Inviting community members to become active at the committee level where they can contribute their time and expertise as they learn more about the organization is an excellent way to prepare them for possible board involvement.

Drawing from your committee membership can be a great method of developing the board in a way that both complements and enhances the group. However, each individual must also meet the specific needs identified by the board through a careful assessment of the organization's strengths and weaknesses.

#123.   **What is founders' syndrome?**

This is a problem that many start-up nonprofits find themselves facing: Original founders remain in positions of authority longer than is necessary. It's important to address this issue as your nonprofit grows—if you broaden the circle of people with decision-making authority, everyone (including your founders) will be much better off.

#124.   **How do I assess the immediate needs of my nonprofit for board development?**

Board development provides an ideal opportunity for self-reflection. It is a way to re-engage the broader community, your supporters, and your colleagues and to gain their insight and opinions about the group's overall goals and the people you need to help you realize those goals.

The immediate needs of most start-up nonprofits generally fall into two areas: finances and staffing. There never seems to be enough money to get everything done, and everyone already has too much work to do. Step back and assess the makeup of your board, where your organization is in relation to your personal needs, and how those elements are affecting the organization's programming and mission. Once you have articulated those elements, you will be well on your way to understanding the nonprofit's current situation.

Assessing the group's immediate needs may require your board members to decide if they are happy with how the organization is being received in the community. As problems are expressed, find out how these issues might be improved. A discussion of your current needs will lead directly to a discussion about future needs and plans to address them. This is not a time to be overly deferential or to avoid making judgments based on experiences and observations that may seem harsh.

Every group has its own set of variables, so there is never a perfect time to assess your organization. You should schedule a formal assessment every year. It does not have to be a complicated undertaking, but it should be clearly defined. All board members, your board administrator (if you have one), and senior volunteers or staff should actively participate.

An assessment can be as simple as making lists of what seems to be working and what needs improvement, and encouraging everyone to offer as much detail as possible. Assessments can take place as part of an already scheduled meeting, at a special session, or even by mail. How you choose to do it is not as important as the fact that you are willing to do it.

#125.   How do I assess the future needs of my nonprofit for board development?

The most exciting part of board development is stepping back now and then to take in the broader view. Think about where your current board wants to take the organization and exactly what types of skills and experiences you will need in new board members to help you get there.

Although no list will cover every nonprofit organization in the country, use the following ideas as an example of the backgrounds and professional training that would be an asset to any organization. You will always need to recognize any conflicts of interest that may arise and take appropriate steps to defuse them. Examine your business plans, budgets, and long-range goals with an eye toward locating the future board members who will help drive the efforts of your organization to reach those goals.

Board of Directors Dream Team

Long-Term Plan	Potential Board Member
Purchasing Property	Real-Estate Agent
Building or Remodeling	General Contractor
Raising Money	Investment Banker
Producing Concerts or Recitals	Promoter or Artist Representative
Increased Involvement in Health Care	Physician, Hospital Administrator, or HMO Representative
Zoning Changes	Lawyer
Increased Fundraising	Foundation Program Officer
Media Sponsorship	Columnist or TV Personality

#126.   **What is a conflict of interest for a board member?**

The best way to understand conflicts of interest is to look at an example—let's pretend you are considering a potential board member named Ms. Jones. She is a highly respected real-estate attorney who would be a tremendous resource on the board for her contacts and business relationships in the community. Ms. Jones owns a few small rental properties around town, one of which is being considered for the organization's new headquarters. In this situation, Ms. Jones would become the group's landlord and benefit financially if the group decided to rent her building, so she needs to sit out all discussions on this particular topic and she should not vote.

Conflicts of interest will inevitably arise, but the knowledge and experience your board members bring to the organization far outweigh the minor inconveniences such conflicts cause.

#127.   **What is board governance?**

Governance involves all the actions that set policy, hire staff, oversee the budget, and generally keep the organization humming along. Fundraising efforts might involve governance from the board as well. The board must mandate systems and put budgets in place before the organization can solicit funds. However, actual fundraising is a standalone activity, generally with its own board committee, processes, and personnel.

#128.   **Should the board connect with other nonprofits?**

There is a huge, wonderful community of nonprofit organizers and groups doing good work, and they are generally more than happy to help the boards of other nonprofits. It is no secret that the entire nonprofit sector of our economy becomes stronger and more vibrant when nonprofits form working alliances and collaborate with one another.

Among nonprofits, cooperation and mutual support are vital. Connecting with others in similar situations will enhance your networking opportunities, which will lead to additional funding streams and increased capacity. You will soon recognize other organizations as allies—not rivals—in your community. Of course, there is competition for some funding, but as you become more established in your niche, your relationships with funders who are interested in your unique mission will solidify, lessening the sense that you are competing against other organizations.

#129. How do I recruit from other nonprofits?

As you think about expanding your board, check out the boards of other organizations. Learn which board members' terms may be expiring and find out who may have an interest in joining your board. An individual with experience as a nonprofit board member is valuable to your organization, especially if she or he meets your board's current needs.

Don't limit yourself to building relationships only with organizations that have identical or similar missions. The purpose of developing these relationships is to help at the board level, not necessarily with programming or operational issues. The mission of a school for homeless kids may be very different from a school teaching creative dance, but at the board level they share similar needs, perhaps related to capital improvements, zoning, and administrative staffing.

#130. What kind of education should the board receive?

New board members generally arrive with either a passion for the organization's mission or because of their stature and connections within the community. They should also meet the criteria you established for new board members and share a profound interest in the group's mission.

Because they will arrive at that first meeting as a blank slate, you need to provide basic education. They must learn about the inner workings of your organization, even if they have experience on other boards or have been involved in other capacities with your organization for years. A carefully chosen board may need to be educated about the details they will be working with, so time spent bringing everyone up to speed is a positive, long-term investment.

One way to educate your board is through board retreats. These provide an opportunity for a crash course about the organization, board member responsibilities, and miscellaneous housekeeping details. During a retreat, encourage members to envision a future for the organization and brainstorm ways to meet goals.

A number of national organizations offer a wide array of classes and seminars designed for nonprofit board members. These programs try to meet the needs of board members at every stage of their personal and organizational development, with offerings that include pending federal legislation affecting tax codes, funding ideas, and learning to work with a group of strangers. Many organizations offer partial scholarships for board members of smaller organizations.

#131. How do I make sure the board reflects the diversity of the community?

A large part of successful nonprofit board development is understanding your service area or client base and then making a commitment to reflect it in your board.

This may be some of the most difficult but necessary work you will do. This aspect of board development requires you to trust yourself, your mission, and your organization enough to welcome people whose gender, race, ethnicity, and life experiences closely reflect your neighborhood and general population onto your board.

At the core of any successful, respected nonprofit is the belief that it is serving the community and is a part of that community. Making a conscious, determined effort to diversify your board will speak volumes about your intentions to do good work as you move forward.

#132. Should the board undergo diversity training?

Incorporating diversity training into long-range planning helps many organizations gain insight into how they function in their communities. Develop a program to move the group toward becoming a more inclusive organization. When these programs are planned in collaboration with your board, they can be a lot of fun as well as educational.

#133. What is an executive director?

The executive director in a nonprofit maintains complete oversight of all operational components and is responsible for all paid or volunteer staff. The board of directors hires the executive director and he or she remains responsible to them. The director's main task, with the cooperation and assistance of the staff, is turning the board's policy directives into programs. The executive director is one of the main people to speak for the organization in the community, so she must have a full and complete understanding of every possible element.

#134. What are the duties of an executive director?

The job description for an executive director, while addressing details specific to your organization, includes these essential duties:

- Is responsible for overall operations, asset protection, and marketing/public relations
- Oversees all accounting functions, including those necessary for auditing, budgeting, financial analysis, capital asset and property management, and payroll in accordance with generally accepted accounting principles
- Handles or delegates all aspects of human resource management, including but not limited to hiring and termination, developing position descriptions, setting compensation, and applying board-approved employee policies and benefits in accordance with federal and state requirements
- Interacts with other personnel and organizations, such as local, county, or state governments, business associations, trade and professional associations, and others
- Assists in the development of current and long-term organizational goals and objectives as well as policies and procedures for operations
- Establishes plans to achieve the goals set by the board of directors and implements policies, subject to approval by the board

#135. **What are the duties of a nonprofit's administrative assistant?**

An administrative assistant works closely with the executive director. This position will become a necessity when your organization reaches a level of maturity that requires hiring an individual who is able to provide support to the director, other professional staff, and the board of directors. A professional in his own right, the administrative assistant will be the first face and voice of the organization that many donors, prospective donors, and members of the general public will encounter. Your group will have its own specific needs for an administrative assistant, but some general duties are:

- Provides executive-level support as required by the executive director and other professional staff
- Prepares agendas and any material needed for general organization meetings, records the minutes of the meetings, and transcribes and distributes the minutes in a timely manner
- Processes organization correspondence—both hard copy and e-mail
- Assists with Internet research on current and prospective donors, entering collected data into the database and creating unique donor profiles
- Staffs events and receptions

#136. What is a board liaison?

A board liaison is the contact between the members of the board and the staff, both paid and volunteer. Individually and as a group, the board has a tremendous amount of time and resources (possibly including money) invested in the organization, and the members will want to be involved directly in day-to-day activities. Boards bring in executive directors to handle these operations, but they still want that hands-on feeling.

For this position, communication strengths are essential. The liaison must keep all lines of communication flowing smoothly so that everyone feels informed, even if she or he is not directly involved in a particular issue.

In collaboration with the administrative assistant, the board liaison also helps prepare all necessary materials for the board members prior to their meetings and assists the committees on an as-needed basis. The board liaison is also responsible for developing board retreats and any other special meetings involving board development. Working in a unique zone among staff, volunteers, and the board, the liaison has the freedom to develop longer-range thinking that will help the board do its work.

#137. **What is a development director?**

The development director is responsible for creating and then implementing the overall fundraising plan for the organization. This position involves a lot more than applying for grants, though grant writing is often an important part of the job. The development director is one of the few positions that do not require daily interaction with other staff members, making it ideal for telecommuting. Files and hard copies of applications should be kept in a central office, but the actual work can be done anywhere there is a computer with access to the Internet.

The development director must be completely comfortable talking to strangers, colleagues, other organizations, and business groups about the organization and its development efforts. In light of the global economic crisis, many of the usual rules and methods for nonprofit development are being revised, so development directors must be able to adjust and adapt.

Nonprofit development has become a highly sought-after position, with people learning the intricacies of the job for many years before taking on the full workload. It is also a position with tremendous responsibilities. If general operating funds are in jeopardy, the development director may have to find new funding sources. General duties include the following:

- Plans and administers all fundraising programs and activities
- Oversees the development department, ensuring staffs and systems operate smoothly and within budget
- Administers annual membership of the organization, including membership drives and solicitations
- Develops and coordinates all capital campaigns for building, expansion, and other programs
- Produces and provides regular detailed accountability reports on finances and fundraising operations
- Offers creative and active leadership for the organization at large

- Spearheads efforts to identify and obtain individual, corporate, and foundation contributions
- Produces proposals, sponsorship invitations, and requests for grants for procuring funds for organizational efforts and causes
- Oversees preparation and production of all promotional mailings, printed pieces, and web communications related to fundraising
- Solicits and cultivates strategic donors
- Devises and executes annual fundraising plans, special events, and programs
- Directs appreciation mailings for all donors
- Serves as a fundraising liaison with the organization's board of directors
- Oversees special events such as auctions and house parties

#138. What is a volunteer coordinator?

A volunteer coordinator needs to enjoy working with all types of people and understands your organization and its mission. The coordinator is often the first point of contact when someone calls or drops by offering to help, so a person able to provide an immediate feeling of welcoming and support will go a long way in recruitment and retention of your volunteer base.

The volunteer coordinator's first responsibility will be to get people registered and entered into your general database. The registration form should include questions about the person's particular interests or skills. Then the coordinator must match those skill sets with the needs of the group. To allow for scheduling, she must communicate regularly with everyone involved in operations to determine what the need for volunteers will be on any given day.

General duties of the volunteer coordinator include:

- Continually seeking new sources for volunteer recruitment

- Preparing material describing volunteer responsibilities
- Interviewing, selecting, and placing qualified individuals in the organization
- Planning and implementing volunteer training programs
- Keeping accurate records of volunteer service time
- Keeping volunteers motivated and enthusiastic

#139. How do volunteers fit in as staff?

Volunteers are the lifeblood of every nonprofit organization. Without people who are willing and able to give freely of their time and expertise, the vast majority of nonprofits would either cease to exist or be so limited in their ability to fulfill their mission that they might as well close their doors.

In the beginning, as you are getting the group up and functioning, everyone will volunteer their time. In time, as the group begins to mature and revenue increases, volunteers may start taking on regular staffing roles, and you may be able to compensate some people. Until then, volunteers will be responsible for running a large part of the organization.

#140. How should I recognize volunteers' contributions?

Always thank them and recognize how essential their contributions are. Having a party to stuff and mail a few thousand envelopes may seem boring, but when everyone remembers why those envelopes are going out—to bring in more people to make the organization grow—the value of their time becomes clear.

Organize special events from time to time. They do not need to be elaborate, but they must take place. Establishing the bond between the organization and its volunteers is one of the benefits of the nonprofit sector, and it is too often overlooked.

#141.   **How do I recruit volunteers?**

The organization's website and newsletter are among the most useful tools to find new volunteers. Preparing notices for submission to the newsletter will keep the need for volunteers on people's minds and will return good results. If you are having trouble getting good volunteers from your existing membership, ask the local service organizations. Many of these organizations try to place their members into volunteer positions in local nonprofits as a way of contributing to the community. Likewise, many larger businesses have in-house programs to help their employees locate volunteer opportunities. These options generally bring out highly skilled, motivated individuals who will be delighted at the opportunity to work with your group.

#142.   **How should my organization participate in special events?**

Getting involved in existing events or starting one on your own is one of the best ways to let your community know what you are doing and why you are doing it. As a nonprofit organization, you may qualify for reduced fees to participate in existing events, so make sure to tell the event coordinators a little bit about your group.

Producing any type of event on your own is going to require a lot of work, so take a good look at your current capacity before committing the group to something that you may not have enough people to organize.

Here are a few examples of special events to consider:

- *Craft/street fairs.* They usually have an area set aside for nonprofit groups.
- *Special events at your local mall or shopping center.* Ask for the mall's Calendar of Events.

- *Business organizations' meet and greets.* Usually held monthly, these events will always welcome new organizations as guests until you are able to join.
- *Open houses.* Throw open your doors and invite the neighborhood in for beverages and conversation.
- *Film nights.* Feature a movie associated with your mission.
- *Co-sponsorship of events produced by other organizations.* This keeps your name visible and shows you are working with more established organizations.

#143. What is the role of an accountant in a nonprofit?

The staff accountant or bookkeeper is responsible for day-to-day financial operations. This person will regularly communicate with the executive director and the treasurer, keeping everyone current on the financial health of the group. Much of the responsibility for accounting in a nonprofit is identical to that in any business; the main differences lie in the state and federal reporting requirements. With a solid background and understanding of accounting principles, that dissimilarity is rarely a problem.

Accounting software such as QuickBooks is the de facto norm, making financial data and recordkeeping uniform throughout many businesses. Your accountant/bookkeeper will handle most of the day-to-day business with your bank, from deposits to payroll. Depending on your organization and the amount of cash involved, he or she will also handle receipts and be responsible for entering and reconciling accounts.

General requirements of a nonprofit organization's accountant include:

- Communicates information and ideas in such a way so others will understand
- Realizes that others in the organization may have limited understanding of what an accountant does

- Has a working knowledge of accounting software and is able to generate reports and run detailed queries
- Possesses a general understanding of what a nonprofit organization is

#144.   **What is a program/project coordinator?**

Coordinators who handle specific projects your organization undertakes can be a huge staffing issue. In the early stages of your nonprofit, the core of your group and your trusted volunteers will coordinate projects.

As you continue to grow, however, the workload may be too large, and it may become necessary to hire someone to coordinate a particular project or event. Although coordinators can be board members who organize committees for the sole purpose of moving a project forward, sometimes it is easier to outsource the task and make it an official job position.

The responsibilities assumed by the ideal project coordinator will depend on the project. It will be necessary to have a core knowledge base relevant to the project before anything else can be considered. If you are establishing an inner-city dental clinic, you will be seeking someone far different than a coordinator for bird-watching field trips as part of an avian society. However, there are some general elements that will apply across the spectrum.

A project coordinator should:

- Have a basic familiarity with budgeting principles and grant writing
- Possess skills in Microsoft Word, Excel, and Power-Point (or the OpenOffice equivalents)
- Have excellent organizational and communication skills (verbal and written)
- Be self-motivated and able to work with minimal supervision

- Understand and have experience working in resource-scarce environments
- Be flexible regarding working hours

#145. **Should nonprofit staff be compensated?**

Brand-new nonprofits are rarely in a position to pay anyone right away. If this is the case with your organization, don't worry.

In time, the workload and associated time commitments will stretch your volunteer base to its limit. Before you reach that point, you must think about compensation for a few people and put those figures into your budget.

There are two important details that everyone involved in the hiring process must understand, regardless of the position and the compensation package:

1. The salary you offer must be a fixed amount
2. Your pay structure must be in line with the community—in other words, no excessive compensation

#146. **Can compensation be tied to performance?**

In nonprofits, all salaries must be fixed numbers, not changeable figures based on "how well we do this year." Tying pay to the organization's performance gives the impression that the employee is personally benefiting from the organization, which is not permitted under IRS law. Such an arrangement would potentially jeopardize your nonprofit status. Although this kind of pay structure is perfectly acceptable in the for-profit world, it is not allowed in a nonprofit. You and your employees need to agree on a set fee and factor that into your overall operating budget.

#147.   **What are the problems with excessive compensation?**

A report of your organization paying excessive compensation is not the type of publicity you want to see on your local television news program. Remember, the public is supporting your non-profit, either by contributions or because your organization does not pay income tax, so they do not want to see employees profiting handsomely.

There are no hard and fast rules to determine what constitutes excessive compensation, which makes it a complex topic. If your pay structure clearly exceeds a comparable position in the community, you are crossing the line. You need to understand what compensation norms are in your area and use them as your guide.

#148.   **Why does conflict occur between operations staff and the board?**

The people who are drawn to the operations side of any organization are invariably different than those who are drawn to the policy-making side. The difference in their goals and methods needs to be recognized and acknowledged for the health of the organization.

Some of the conflict surfaces because the board is made up of volunteers who may attend only a few meetings a month yet feel the need to stay involved in day-to-day operations. Naturally, they want to shepherd and nurture an organization they feel strongly about, and you should respect this. However, board members also need to trust the people who are responsible for the daily running of the organization.

The operations staff may have a better view of how policies impact the community the organization exists to serve, and they may be frustrated by their inability to make changes they know are needed. This is why establishing firm lines of communication and developing mutual respect between the board of directors and the operations staff is crucial.

#149. Should staff members attend board meetings?

Although most staff people dislike attending board meetings, extend the invitation now and then. People who say they don't like meetings may actually be saying that they don't understand what is going on and feel out of place.

Assure them that they don't have to participate; they can simply observe and get a feel for the dynamics of the board of directors. If they have questions, encourage them to ask them after the meeting. At the meeting, introduce the guests in the room and let the meeting progress as usual.

#150. How should board members reach out to staff and volunteers?

Encourage board members to spend time with the volunteers or staff, helping in a hands-on way with the real work of the organization. This will help the board understand the staff's frustrations and worries, as well as experience the joy of direct work within the community.

In a similar vein, it may be beneficial for board members to be available for informal conversations with staff and volunteers who may be having trouble or need a little help. The board members made it onto your board because they brought clearly identifiable talents or resources to the organization. Although most of their time may be committed to board functions, your organization can only benefit if they are also of direct assistance to the larger group. This is not an invitation to meddle or micromanage; instead, it is an opportunity to offer wisdom and knowledge with the luxury of being removed from the ongoing work.

#151.   How can committees help with conflict?

Working, active, and engaged committees that grow out of the board of directors are often the hidden strength of nonprofit organizations. Creating a supportive committee structure that encourages board members and community members to assume governance responsibilities provides an outlet for creative ideas and helps funnel those ideas into productive actions without cluttering up already full workloads. Many of the stresses that come from having either a detached board or too many people involved in making operational decisions can be alleviated by making certain the committees are up and running.

#152.   How do I define board oversight?

The board must remain focused on the big-picture issues that affect the organization. Board oversight involves ongoing communications with major donors and others in the community who feel comfortable only when they are dealing directly with a board member.

It is also good for individual board members to know that one of the most important contributions they can make to the organization is to maintain their strong connections within the broader community.

There is a fine line between being a board member with an eye on the big picture and one who thinks she is in charge. Board members who find themselves on the wrong side of that line can inadvertently cause serious problems, even in well-established organizations. Staff and board members must develop a mutually respectful relationship. They must recognize one another's strengths and build an atmosphere of trust.

Far too many organizations have fallen victim to internal conflicts. These can be avoided when everyone understands how they fit into the overall organization, are comfortable with it, and trust everyone else involved.

#153. **How should financial responsibility be shared?**

To a large degree, the financial responsibility for the organization will be a shared responsibility. Even so, you need clearly defined roles to avoid conflict. In the start-up phase, the board president, the treasurer, and the person who is overseeing day-to-day operations need to collaborate to develop the budget. An executive director, if you have one, must be directly involved with the board members to provide the real-world guidance they may need.

For the budget to work, everyone must understand that a fine line exists between cooperation and micromanaging. It is time to choose the best people for the tasks at hand. The monthly board meeting is the traditional time to discuss the financial health of the organization. If you are using standard accounting software, monthly financial statements are a simple matter to produce, but there is no guidance on interpretation.

#154. **Should a staff member or board member present financial information?**

Many organizations have a staff person present financial updates to the board, either in a narrative form or with copies of the financial documentation produced using accounting software such as QuickBooks.

This reporting method is not without problems. It can go right over the heads of board members who may not have been following the operations as closely as staff does. It also places an artificial barrier between the board and the staff person who presents the information precisely when all barriers need to be removed so that honest assessments can take place. The monthly reporting needs to be as free as possible from potential conflict.

An excellent alternative is to have the treasurer, a member of the board, open the conversation by presenting the report. This option offers a level playing field for the board to discuss finances, since the information is presented to them by a peer.

Of course, the treasurer needs to be conversant with the details of the budget and must know how to read a spreadsheet in order to lead the discussion. Discuss who should present the financials with the board and with any staff directly involved in preparing the monthly reports. This strategy enables you to reach a decision that meets everyone's needs.

#155.   What is programming?

Programming covers everything the public sees, such as the services your group provides, the classes you run, or the lecture series you present. It is your public face in the community; it defines who you are. Programming should follow the broad, general outlines developed by the board, but it is executed by the staff in their operations capacity. Programming and budget go hand in hand, so you can never consider one without looking at the other.

#156.   How do I create a multiyear programming plan?

A multiyear plan that outlines your programming goals will give your members and the community a clear sense of your plans and intentions. The plan does not need to be complex, but it should identify fully achievable goals in one-, three-, and five-year sections. The plan needs to be coordinated with sources of projected and realistically expected funding, such as membership dues, fees for service or grants, and other sources. List only your realistic expectations that have a planned funding stream in place.

#157. **How do I use planned series programs?**

Developing your long-range programming around any number of "series" is one way to expand a small start-up program plan into a multiyear cycle. For example, if a class is held three times a year, draw up a prospective schedule that stretches three to five years into the future. Selecting approximate dates and times for the classes shows the planned continuity of your programming. This becomes very important when talking with potential funders, and it is also a good way to keep your board interested and your staff motivated.

#158. **What is the importance of the board liaison?**

The duties of the board liaison were outlined in Question #136, but it is important to note that bringing on a board liaison may be among the best personnel decisions your organization will ever make. It makes little difference if that person is compensated or volunteers his or her time. The ability to funnel ideas and process through one central point has saved many start-up nonprofits from an early demise. The liaison's immediate task is essentially clerical. She must obtain and update the contact information for the board and everyone involved in your group's operations. Much of the role will be to facilitate ongoing, open communication, so having all necessary contact information is important.

The liaison should also be involved in building the agenda for your monthly board meetings, which will require access to the operational documents and materials in process. Likewise, the board needs to become comfortable addressing operational inquiries to the liaison, as well as raising financial questions so they can be folded into any discussions that are to take place. When practical, the board liaison should attend meetings of the board's standing committees, not as a board member or staff member but as a liaison, working equally with all the groups that make up the organization.

#159.   What are the benefits of an open-door policy?

An open-door policy can help maintain a positive, upbeat feeling throughout the organization. People have different roles and responsibilities, but to maintain a smoothly running organization, the lines of communication must be as open and free-flowing as possible. An open-door policy is the operational equivalent of maintaining transparency.

When people know that nothing is being kept from them, they will remember why they chose to work together to form or join the organization. They will be less likely to get bogged down in petty disagreements. If you choose, include the policy in the bylaws. The only possible limitations to an open-door policy will occur when dealing with the following:

- *Pending legal issues.* If your organization is involved in any type of legal action, do not broadcast the information.
- *Personnel issues.* Any discussion of salaries, professional reviews, or issues surrounding a termination should be confidential.
- *Real-estate transactions.* Until a deal is final, any number of things can upset ongoing negotiations, so these should not be shared with everyone.

#160.   Why are people drawn to work for nonprofits?

There is something unique about working for a nonprofit. Whether or not pay is involved, nonprofits seem to attract a wonderful group of people. These are individuals who apply themselves to organizations that all too often struggle financially.

People such as you are drawn to nonprofits because you believe more deeply in the mission of the organization than in a desire to gain great wealth. Of course, positions with nonprofits are real jobs with real responsibilities. However, taking the profit motive out of the picture makes it possible to devote yourself to the actual work without focusing on the bottom line.

There is also a sense of ownership unlike anything you'll encounter in a for-profit business. Working at a nonprofit often becomes much more than just another job. The mission—the core of the organization—is the driving force in all aspects of the organization. It affects all who work or volunteer their time.

There is a very deep sense of pride that comes from working—either for pay or as a volunteer—for most nonprofit organizations. People love to share the achievements in which they have been involved—for example, the opening of a community garden, working in a small art school, or protecting an ancient forest from development. As outsiders learn about an organization's mission and the good work it does, they want to be a part of it as well.

#161. Can clients become staff?

In the for-profit world, it's rare that a customer will actually buy a company. However, it's by no means unheard of in nonprofits for clients to become staff or volunteers. A person who brings lost animals to a shelter may wind up volunteering a few hours a month behind the desk, or the parent of a kid in a nonprofit summer camp may become an instructor in that camp.

Because of the special relationships nonprofits can establish in a community, the traditional lines between service beneficiary and service provider blur. Unless there are clear conflicts of interest, which normally won't be an issue unless the roles involve board membership, there is no problem with people who were previously clients taking on different roles within the organization.

#162.   **What is a personnel committee?**

Many organizations form a personnel committee to handle the human resource issues that may arise. Although this is a committee of the board, its membership can include anyone the board chooses. Unlike other committees, personnel meetings are rarely open. Deliberations are not reported in the general board minutes but in confidential reports to the board.

There are many reasons for confidentiality when dealing with personnel issues. First, you must always respect the feelings and reputation of an employee who may be having a difficult time with issues unrelated to the organization but that are affecting performance. In addition, if the personnel committee also acts as a hiring committee, it is inappropriate to divulge names of people you chose not to hire. These people may be members of your community, and announcing that they were not hired would cause, at the very least, embarrassment and, at the worst, serious harm to their reputation.

The second and most important reason to maintain confidentiality is the threat of lawsuits. Employee-related lawsuits represent the greatest need for board and officer insurance. Like it or not, people often pursue legal action when calm negotiation or binding arbitration would have resolved the problem.

#163.   **What type of employee policies should be in place?**

Before it can make any hiring decisions, the personnel committee usually must draft and submit an employee manual for approval by the full board of directors. There are many examples from other nonprofits on which to base such a manual. Include a welcoming page from the director or board president. A new volunteer or paid employee will be nervous in the beginning, and reading a friendly note from the people at the very core of the organization will ease the transition into the group.

The first major section of the handbook should contain employee policies. These policies inform employees and volunteers what you expect of them. Cover details such as schedules, use of the computer, and confidentiality issues. This is also the best place to spell out the general expectations the organization has for everyone, volunteer or paid staff. This may include the mission statement or other documents that explain why the organization exists.

The handbook is also the place for general housekeeping details such as hours of operation, recognized holidays, and basic procedures. If compensated personnel are involved, include details about pay and benefits.

#164. **How should I deal with employee grievances and reviews?**

The personnel committee should arbitrate problems that will inevitably arise among your staff members. A committee consisting of people representing many parts of the organization often encourages an increased level of openness not possible in traditional employee/employer meetings. Minor grievances can be resolved painlessly as soon as people are comfortable and begin to talk. Situations that are very serious or complicated will require outside help or mediation to resolve. For most situations in small nonprofit organizations just starting out, few problems will accelerate to a level that requires such intervention.

Weekly or monthly staff meetings for everyone involved in operations are essential. Having the opportunity to talk with and listen to one another often resolves potentially problematic situations long before they escalate. Remember that your volunteers are every bit as important as any paid staff and should be included in meetings or other communications. The reliance on volunteers is a two-way street; they give you their time and expertise, and you must give them respect and gratitude for their hard work.

#165. **What is the role of a code of conduct in a nonprofit?**

The code of conduct in a nonprofit must reflect and represent the very best of who you are. As a publicly supported entity, your inner workings are mostly exposed. How you decide to articulate acceptable (and, conversely, unacceptable) behavior by everyone involved in the organization speaks volumes about who you are.

Post the code of conduct in a public place where it is visible to anyone in your organization as well as to members of the general public. It is a reminder of what types of behavior are acceptable and what types of behavior are not tolerated. Over time, some parts of the code of conduct may not work, may seem out of touch, or may need to be changed. Bring up the code and invite input at staff meetings, committee meetings, or even larger organizational meetings. If changes are necessary, propose these adjustments to the board.

#166. **What is the role of an independent contractor in a nonprofit's staff?**

At some point, your organization will need outside help for tasks that are beyond the capabilities of the volunteer pool. You will have to decide whether to employ people or hire them as independent contractors. There are advantages and disadvantages to either option, and you may have to consider some ethical questions. Businesses in the for-profit sector also face these questions, but the difference lies in how and why you make these decisions.

An independent contractor is a private business of one person. By signing a legally binding contract, that person agrees to provide a specific service to your organization for a set fee.

The electrician who rewired the office and the webmaster who maintains your website are examples of independent contractors. They agreed to perform a service, you paid them, and that was the end of the story. The individuals may have been employed by a company—perhaps an Internet service provider or an electrical service company—but in their working relationship with your organization, they were contractors.

This situation is far different from contracting with someone to handle a task on an ongoing basis. A one-time independent contractor is only committed for a set period of time or until a specific task is completed.

The contractor rarely receives benefits such as health insurance, is often responsible for her own taxes, and is not eligible for unemployment compensation. This arrangement can be a major disadvantage for the contractor, but it can be an advantage for the organization that hires her.

#167. **What is the role of a traditional employee in a nonprofit's staff?**

If you are uncomfortable with the idea of hiring independent contractors, there is another option: hire an individual as an employee following a process identical to that used by for-profit companies. As an employer, your organization becomes responsible for payroll withholdings for taxes and social security and can offer health insurance, if that is an option. Federal and state labor laws immediately cover the new employee; these laws exist as a baseline for issues ranging from minimum wages to required hours to holidays.

A negotiated contract can outline all the particulars and responsibilities of both the employee and the organization. Hiring employees inevitably means more complex bookkeeping, so anticipate the need for a competent, professional bookkeeper.

#168. **What does "exempt employee" mean?**

An "exempt employee" usually refers to a salaried employee, that is, someone who does not work by the hour and therefore is not eligible for overtime pay. Speak to a lawyer who has a background in employment law if you have any questions about how your employees should be classified.

#169. **What is collective bargaining?**

Collective bargaining is the good-faith process between an employer or management and a trade union representing the employees. It is the process for negotiating wages, responsibilities, working hours, working conditions, and other details that affect what the employees do and how the interaction between the employees and the organization moves forward.

Collective bargaining is the fundamental principle on which the trade union system is based. On the surface, collective bargaining in the context of a nonprofit is not different from any other labor negotiations. But dig a little deeper, and things can be very different.

#170. **What is the right to organize?**

American labor law makes very few distinctions between for-profit and nonprofit businesses. A number of national organizations that represent many classifications of workers are actively organizing individuals in the nonprofit sector. This has generally been a positive trend for the employees and, ultimately, for the organizations in which they work.

#171. **What is the role of confrontation in nonprofits?**

Many for-profit businesses were founded and continue to thrive in a highly competitive environment where intense negotiations and confrontations are necessary. Prevailing in such an environment is part of doing business, but many people who are drawn to nonprofits feel differently.

For-profit and nonprofit businesses function differently in terms of how the negotiating parties view each other and how they arrive at a fair and equitable contract. In nonprofits, many employees have a deep emotional bond with the mission of the organization and naturally seek consensus over confrontation, so the idea of a labor-bargaining session can be upsetting.

A number of forward-thinking unions are recognizing the differences between nonprofit workplaces and companies in the for-profit sector. They are learning to work for the good of both the workers and the organization, seeking a win-win outcome.

Chapter 10

NONPROFIT AS BUSINESS

#172. Does my nonprofit need a business plan?

When most people think of a business plan, they think in terms of a plan geared to a for-profit company. But nonprofits need business plans too. A business plan shows potential funders how you intend to carry out your operational goals. It will also be an important part of the 1023 form (see Chapter 12) you submit to the IRS when applying for nonprofit status.

#173. What does the business plan need to include?

The core elements and terminology of a complete for-profit or non-profit business plan are very similar. There are ingredients that any potential funder will expect to see, and you need to include them.

The cover sheet or executive summary will be the first page the reader will see, but it should be the last page you write. It is a summary of what is to come, so wait until your business plan has been fully developed and you know exactly what your cover sheet should say. Keep your sentences short and to the point, but explain who you are, what your company or organization intends to do, and how you plan to do it. No potential funders are going to make a decision based on this summary alone. However, they may decide to continue reading based on what you write here.

The next section should be your statement of purpose or mission statement. It must clearly describe the services you provide to the community and the passion of the individuals involved in your organization.

After the mission statement should be the table of contents. This will provide an immediate guide, which the reader can also use to locate specific data. If you are writing for online distribution, use the table-of-contents function in most word processing programs, which enables a quick jump to specific sections. If you are planning to print a hard copy, be careful to cancel that option so you don't have the hyperlink lines running through your document.

Next up is a description of your business. Make the description of your business or organization clear and concise—no longer than a paragraph. Many details that might fit in the description will appear in detail elsewhere in the plan.

After this should come an outline of your marketing plans. Marketing, particularly when applied to nonprofits, means fully understanding the needs of your clients or community and then managing your organizational response to meet those needs. It is not simply your publicity efforts, although they may play a role in it. Attach any informational brochures or other outreach material you have developed for general reference.

Here is where you mention any use of focus groups to help you evaluate how well the marketing is working or where improvements may be necessary. Be sure to indicate who is conducting the groups and how frequently they will occur (focus groups are probably something you'll want to outsource to a dedicated vendor). Likewise, identify by name who is directly involved in or leading your marketing strategy.

Next, you need to discuss the competition your organization may be facing. Be honest in your analysis and point out exactly how your organization will be different and why that difference deserves to be funded.

The next section should describe your operating procedures. Here you may want to attach or reference your bylaws. The point of this section is to help the reader fully understand how your organization functions, where the decision-making responsibility is, and what the process is for accountability. If you included clear nondiscriminatory clauses in your bylaws, this is a fine opportunity to share them.

The final section should discuss personnel. This may include your staff and any consultants. List them here with a sentence describing each person's position and qualifications. Resumes or the curriculum vitae of the board members will be included later as supporting documents.

You want to convey that your organization has good, competent people in positions of responsibility. If your organization is fortunate enough to have the services of someone whose name is known throughout the community, mention it in the narrative.

#174.   **What should be included in the supporting financial documents?**

Supporting financial documents are one tier below the general description of who you are and what your organization plans to do. Here you need to provide as much solid documentation as possible to back up the good intentions in the overview.

First up is the breakeven analysis, which explains what the organization is doing to break even. If you are falling short, outline what is planned in the next fiscal year to correct existing problems.

Next is the three-year financial summary. This summary will be similar to that required when you prepare Form 1023 to apply for a tax exemption, if you are going to file before you have a multiyear history. Any standard grant application requires this kind of summary.

If you do not have a three-year financial history, use the pro forma cash-flow document to project estimated income and expenses that you are confident the organization will have, but you do not as yet have the hard numbers to back up the calculations.

Pro forma means "as if" and is used when you need to discuss funds that do not exist yet, but you are confident that they will.

Next include a balance sheet. This can be a summary of your current fiscal year's budget, or you can attach a more comprehensive document. As with other parts of the plan, be careful not to provide so much information that the reader loses interest.

#175. What should be included in the general supporting documents?

Supporting documents provide the evidence that what you are saying in your business plan is real. These documents are essential to show the depth of your organization. They give a clear picture of who you are and what you are doing in the world. Very few grant-making committees will have the time or inclination to read through pages of documentation. They want to see that your organization has the documents and that they are current, particularly with respect to any financial documentation.

You need to include copies of licenses and all legal documents. The board secretary should have copies of all documents the organization has compiled since the decision to incorporate. For the purpose of the business plan, you will generally need only the cover sheets, because they have the legal date stamp or other indicator that the particular license or permit is valid. Once you have obtained your federal tax exemption, you will only need to present the determination letter to verify your status. Include a copy of the latest Form 990.

You should also include copies of any leases or purchase agreements for business space. These documents show one of the organization's major expenses, one that would obviously affect your ability to function if it were cut. This documentation also points to the current stability of the organization; the fact that the leadership has agreed to a long-term commitment indicates stability.

If you are carrying any type of insurance—for example, property or vehicle insurance or board insurance—you should also include its documentation. This gives the reader a clear picture of your organization. Carrying an insurance policy is evidence that your organization is responsible and that you are taking necessary precautions and limiting unnecessary risks.

You may want to include copies of letters of intent. These copies may be necessary if you want to show that your organization is a viable business with outstanding financial obligations. Letters of intent identify the amount of money you are requesting and fully document the need for those funds. The ability to provide the actual letters of intent from the businesses you are working with and who will ultimately receive the requested funds shows the full and comprehensive nature of your business plan.

In this section you should also include any pending loan applications. This is not money you currently have to work with but rather funds you hope to receive. You include them to present as much information about your business as possible.

The information can be as complete or abbreviated as you are comfortable with, but potential funders need to know the financial health of your organization and be aware of your current loan application(s).

The last item to include is your equipment list. The depreciation of this equipment will appear in your budget, so including it here will show that the entire document is complete.

#176. **What information should I include about my board members?**

Have a one-page resume or curriculum vitae (CV) from each of your board members or, at the very least, from your current officers and any staff with direct responsibility or oversight concerning the organization's finances. Although your group is incorporated and that incorporation entails the legal separation between the individuals and the corporate entity, your business plan is still going to be reviewed by real people.

It is essential that your readers feel comfortable enough with the people who represent your organization to make a financial contribution. Although there will be opportunities for in-person meetings, everyone involved at this stage will base their decisions on the paperwork on the table, and that paperwork must show your organization in its finest light and prove that the people running it have the experience to make everything work.

#177. **What are the main differences between a nonprofit business plan and a for-profit business plan?**

The biggest difference, of course, is how you handle any money above the amount that is necessary to operate the organization. Many of the terms used in a for-profit business plan need to be adjusted to accommodate the unique situation of a nonprofit. These subtle edits are necessary to appreciate the differences between for-profit and nonprofit business plans and the terminology used for each.

- *Customers Become Clients:* This is a subtle but essential change in terminology. You are crafting a business plan whose focus is on returning funds to the organization to further its mission rather than returning profits to investors or increasing the profit margin.
- *Investors Become Funders:* The idea of investing in a project or an organization comes with an expectation that there will be some form of benefit to the investor in exchange for the money. In a for-profit business, that benefit may take any number of forms, from appointments to high offices to a thank-you payment at the end of the year. However, any of those benefits are illegal in a nonprofit organization because no one is allowed to use the work of the organization for personal gain.

  Any perception of personal gain can jeopardize your tax-exempt status and all the work you have put into developing the organization. People who give money to your organization must be seen as funders who contribute because they feel strongly enough about the merits of the organization's mission to be willing to write a check. The only direct benefit to those funders will be their ability to deduct that contribution from their tax liability; they can expect nothing else from the nonprofit they helped fund.

- *Products Become Programs or Services:* It is entirely appropriate for a for-profit business to create, produce, and sell a product—something of value that can be touched or experienced. Product lines in a for-profit business can be adjusted with very few legal restrictions. The owners are legally free to modify product lines without any explanation. Naturally, there are market limitations and cash-flow issues, but on a basic level, it is unlikely that the IRS will question a decision to change or drastically modify a product line.

  A nonprofit is limited to providing a service that falls within the broad interpretation of its mission. Its tax-exempt status depends entirely on its ability to carry out its stated mission without straying from it.

- *A Profit and Loss Statement Becomes a Statement of Financial Activities:* Profit and loss statements do not appear in the financial documents of a nonprofit, but you need to demonstrate the financial health of the organization. You can do this through a statement of financial activities, a basic document that measures an organization's finances during a specified time. The function of a financial statement is to total all sources of revenue and subtract all expenses related to the revenue.

Having a financial statement prepared on a regular schedule enables the organization to quickly get a sense of its financial health. If the statement points to a problem each month, you will be able to address it before the problem becomes a crisis. Likewise, if the numbers are consistently good, you are doing something right!

#178.   What is the purpose of a nonprofit's mission statement?

In one or two paragraphs, your mission statement explains the core elements of your organization: its purpose, its target population, and its activities. Every nonprofit organization needs a mission statement. The statement may change slightly over time, as the organization adjusts its goals, but it will remain the guiding document for your organization.

#179.   What sort of research should I do when developing my mission statement?

Developing a clear, concise mission statement is difficult, especially when you are working with smart, passionate people who want the very best for the organization. Mission statements are not the depository for the wishes and desires of every person involved in the group; rather, they are a place to distill those ideas to their essence. They need to be presented clearly, concisely, and in a manner that internal or external audiences can easily understand.

A good first step is to do some research. Look at the mission statements of other organizations. Try to understand how the work they do lines up with their mission statement, and look at the methods they use to convey their ideas in a clear manner.

It is also wise to look at the grant applications of potential donors. This research allows you to see exactly what they are seeking and what they want to see in the mission statements of the groups they choose to fund. Private foundations may choose not to reveal the groups and organizations they fund, but government agencies and public charities do. You will find more than enough examples to review.

#180.   Can my mission statement change over time?

Sometimes a group gets stuck or finds it is unable to agree on the precise wording. Sometimes, as your organization grows, your mission may shift, or the way you view the work may adjust. This is completely natural.

If the mission statement is no longer accurate, or the wording you settled on a few months ago is no longer correct, review it and make the needed changes. The adjustments must go through your board of directors, who will very likely have their own input and who need to agree to the changes.

#181.   What is my nonprofit's "vision"?

It's important to define your vision so that people who have never heard of your organization understand what you are doing and are inspired to join your effort. Vision may touch on the underlying beliefs of why you are doing the work you are doing. Faith-based non-profits often weave their core vision into their ongoing work, whereas secular groups may have to start from the beginning to understand and be comfortable articulating the ultimate purpose of their work.

It is not easy to explain your passion for stray animals, forests, the performing arts, or any of the countless other missions the nonprofit community undertakes. However, explain it you must. Articulate it in such a way that the many intended audiences—members, funders, and the general public—will also understand and share that passion.

#182.   What should the mission statement communicate to the general community?

Always remember the audience you are trying to reach. Over time, the members of your core group will understand one another through working and discussion. The mission statement is not the place to talk to yourselves, as fun and as easy as that may be.

You are preparing a document that will be read by people you do not know and may never meet. Do not waste time developing wording that impresses your group. You need to focus on the external audience and how they will read and interpret your words. Most of them will never actually read the mission statement; they don't need to read it. The way your organization functions and the work it does will speak for itself. The mission statement anchors the organization; the organization's purpose stems from its principles.

#183. **What should the mission statement communicate to the nonprofit funding community?**

Potential donors will need time to review material about your organization in order to determine if your work clearly lines up with their philosophies or interests. This is why your mission statement is so important.

The mission statement will be the document most funders need to give them a picture of your group that goes beyond budgets and a business plan. They will learn what makes you tick, what drives the group to take on a task or a project, or why your group is putting everything it has on the line with no expectation of financial reward.

#184. **What are my nonprofit's guiding principles?**

Your guiding principles are simple: to respect other people, to work toward the enhancement of a community or a way of life, and not to engage in mean or violent activities. Although these principles may be second nature to your group, until and unless you state them, no one outside your group is going to realize how you are thinking and how serious and committed you are.

The fact that your organization believes in principles that go far beyond its actual tasks will show the community and the many audiences who might read your mission statement that you are willing to state the beliefs that guide everything in the organization.

#185.   **What is the sticky dot exercise?**

There are a number of exercises to help groups develop their mission statements. The exercises can take place during board retreats, or they can be part of your regularly scheduled meetings. One of these exercises is the sticky dot exercise. You will need butcher paper, a volunteer to act as the writer, and a package of green, yellow, and red colored sticky dots.

Hang the butcher paper on an easel in the front of the room; the writer stands beside the easel. Encourage everyone in the room to call out what they think the real mission of the organization is (or should be!).

There is no right or wrong suggestion. Ideas can be unsurprising or outlandish; the writer should note them all on the butcher paper as clearly as possible in big letters. Don't offer any criticism (and don't allow anyone else to do so), even if a suggestion sounds ridiculous.

After a predetermined time, the writer calls for final suggestions and closes this part of the exercise. It is a good time to take a break and encourage everyone to walk around and look at the suggestions. See which ones make the most sense or reflect each individual's ideas about the organization's true mission.

Now, distribute the sticky dots. Everyone should have an equal assortment of colors. Place the green dots by ideas that you think are appropriate. Place the yellow dots near ideas that are neutral, and the red dots next to suggestions that you can't support. It does not matter who put what colored dot by which suggestion.

At the close of this part of the exercise, the colored sticky dots will clearly tell which elements the group thinks are important enough to include in the mission statement. These suggestions or statements will give the group a clearer understanding of their mission and will find their way into the mission statement.

#186. **What is the round robin table exercise?**

Another potential exercise is the round robin table. The best facilitator for this exercise is an individual who is not directly involved in the organization but who is familiar with developing nonprofit mission statements. Attendees are placed into small groups, ideally at tables that allow them to sit and have room to write.

Each group compiles a list of what they think the organization represents. After a set period, a representative from each table visits the other tables to glean ideas from those groups and take them back to his or her group. Allow plenty of time for the representatives of the different tables to understand the ideas as they are stated as well as any impressions or nuances.

The tables or groups then incorporate their original list of important elements with the other groups' ideas.

After this portion of the exercise, each group reads its final results. With the help of the facilitator, the ideas are merged into a list of elements. This list can be used to draft a rough document, which is then edited and prepared for the board of directors for eventual adoption. Then it will become part of the group's constantly evolving record.

Chapter 11

PUBLICITY AND MARKETING

#187. Does my nonprofit need a website?

Yes. This is not an option; it is a necessity, so take it seriously. The Internet is without question one of the finest tools in any organizer's toolbox, but to be effective your nonprofit must develop and implement an online marketing strategy, including a website.

If your experience with the Internet has been primarily as an end user with an e-mail account or as a casual web surfer, you need a brief overview of how to create a website. Then you will be able to use and share this basic understanding in developing your organization's site.

Your website can serve many purposes, from providing general outreach to boosting fundraising to facilitating internal communications. What you actually want and need, plus what your group is able to pay for, will determine its design.

#188. How should I select a webmaster?

At some point, your organization may have a fully functioning information technology department, but in the beginning, you need to identify and contract with someone who will be able to put together and maintain a website for you. That person is a webmaster.

Your webmaster must obviously understand the technical aspects of the task, but most importantly, she must be able and willing to listen to your wants and needs. You do not want someone who speaks in streams of jargon and expects you to agree.

Since the webmaster will need information relating to both web content and features from the committees as well as the board, having a clear line of communication is essential. Therefore, she should be in regular communication with one board member or a liaison designated by the board. In time, you may incorporate web development into a standing committee, such as publicity or outreach, but when you are trying to get all the essential elements in place, it's fine to have the web functioning ad hoc.

#189. **What are the basic tasks of creating a website?**

Website creation and development is complex and requires a competent professional. As the end user, there are a few things you should do to speed up the process. First, select and register a domain name with any of the main registration companies such as *www.mydomain.com* or *www.godaddy.com.*

Your domain is your address on the Internet. It must be unique (not already taken), easy to remember, and accurately reflect who you are. Your organization's name may still be available, in which case you are set. If it's not, be creative. Once you have a domain name, you must select a web-hosting service.

These services can be free or there may be a monthly charge. First, identify the service you want to use and the amount of money you want to spend, but hold off on doing anything until you have selected a person to put your website together. Next, you must select the software you want to use to author the website. These programs help you put together the actual content that is uploaded to the server. One of the favorite web-development software programs in the nonprofit community is Drupal (*www.drupal.org*), an open-source software (there's no charge) designed for the end user to be able to add to or change content on the website. As with much of the open-source software, the expenses for the end user accumulate during setup and continue with ongoing maintenance and consulting fees. Ask your webmaster exactly what costs you can expect over the course of your contract. Work those projected costs into your yearly budget so there are no surprises.

#190. What type of content should be on my website?

This will be determined to some degree by the program you selected to build the site and your webmaster's ability to adjust that program to meet your specific requests and needs. Possible elements to put on your site include the following:

- An opening/home page introducing your organization
- A blog that is updated on a regular schedule
- A button that allows viewers to make immediate donations
- Links to your committees and board members
- Reciprocal links to organizations and businesses in the community that support your efforts

#191. Should my nonprofit have a newsletter?

Even in this age of instant communication, do not underestimate the importance and value of a well-produced newsletter. You can and should put up a newsletter on your website, but you should also design yours for printing and distribution throughout the community.

Whereas a website requires a person to find you, newsletters are mailed directly to your supporters and distributed throughout the community. They are a proactive means of reaching a new audience wherever they might be. A newsletter can be as simple as a one-page sheet copied on an as-needed basis or as elaborate as a multiple-page tabloid that resembles a newspaper more than a traditional newsletter.

#192. How do I use desktop publishing?

There is a wide range of desktop publishing applications available, and you should take the time to familiarize yourself with them. Some of the software is free, but you can also get high-end programs that cost thousands of dollars. Some form of desktop publishing may have come with your word processing program, so look at what you already have before buying anything.

Most desktop publishing programs include templates for newsletters. Open them up and play with them. Try out the styles and the options until you settle on one that pleases you or your newsletter committee.

#193. What should my newsletter contain?

Be efficient in your use of space. Your viewers will expect to see:

- A monthly calendar of scheduled events
- A directory of the key people in the organization and a synopsis of their responsibilities
- A membership form that can be cut out and mailed if you are a membership organization
- A message from the board president or others who are helping to grow the organization

#194. How do I distribute my newsletter?

Put your newsletter onto your website as soon as it is complete. Mail or deliver printed hard copies to:

- Contributors, members, and interested community members
- Local cafés, community centers, theaters, or other locations appropriate to your organization
- Organizations doing similar work in other parts of the country

#195. Should my organization have a designated media person?

Your organization may find it helpful to select one person to develop contacts and build needed relationships with your local media. Regardless of where you are located, there are numerous media organizations, from free weekly newspapers to the regional television outlets to AM and FM radio stations. Each outlet has staff dedicated to covering local activities. Your media person needs to meet those individuals.

Send this person any press releases or general advisories about things your group is doing, as well as personal invitations to attend your board meetings, tour your facility, or attend one of your events. You want to build a relationship, so that when the media have a question, they will know exactly whom to contact. Likewise, when you have something you think is newsworthy, you will have the right person already in your directory.

#196. How do I create a press release template?

Making a press release template and storing it on the organization's computer will make the task of generating press releases easy, quick, and efficient. The template is only one page and sent on letterhead. You can list Who, What, Where, When, and Why, and fill them in. Do a "save as" for the event or topic of the release and send it to every media outlet in your region. Before long, the media organizations will recognize your press releases and begin giving you necessary coverage.

#197. How should I use fairs and community festivals for publicity?

Community festivals are a terrific opportunity to get out, meet people, and let everyone know what you are doing. People are already in a good mood, so it is easy to engage complete strangers in conversation. There are a few ways to approach local festivals, but the first task is to obtain a comprehensive list of every event in your region, including dates, locations, and contacts.

Every state and most counties operate tourist or visitor information offices. As part of their services, they offer calendars of events for their service areas. Those listings will include every conceivable type of public gathering, many of which might be perfect for your organization to attend. Many festivals make special allowances for nonprofit organizations to have a booth or table at a reduced cost or at no cost, with the stipulation that it is for informational purposes only. This is an excellent opportunity to get your material into the hands of many people in your community, add names to your mailing list, publicize upcoming events, and conduct outreach.

#198. How do I set up a booth at a fair?

If you are only interested in promoting your organization and do not plan to sell anything, a booth at a fair is a wonderful method of outreach, and it's also a lot of fun. You can usually make your newsletter available, invite people to join your mailing list, and generally get the word out to a lot of people in a very short time.

If space is at a premium, consider sharing a booth with other nonprofits. Many long-running craft fairs throughout the country started as and continue to be fundraisers for the sponsoring organization, so the event coordinators know what it's like to be in your position and often have a soft spot for start-up nonprofits.

#199. Should my organization sponsor a stage at a fair?

Many street fairs have outdoor stages where local performers can entertain the crowds throughout the event. If your budget allows, consider sponsoring a stage or helping to underwrite some cost associated with it. In return, your organization will be included in any event publicity, which helps establish your group as a member of the community.

#200. How do I create a mailing list?

In the beginning, your mailing list will be made up of people who were active in the initial formation of the organization. Slowly, that list will grow to include people who have helped in one way or another, including financially. In time, you will find it beneficial to open your general mailing list to anyone who expresses even the slightest interest in what you are doing, and the collection of names will become a high priority. Make sure you have a designated system for taking down the names and contact information of everyone your organization interacts with.

#201. How do I use a mailing list for fundraising?

The greatest fundraising letter in the world will not do much good if you do not have places to send it. Mailing lists are considered money in the bank for many organizations. These lists contain people who came to you; they are already supporters.

Keeping your mailing list on a simple spreadsheet that organizes information about when people joined the list, how you made contact with them, and what, if any, contributions they have made. Obviously, as your organization matures, your fundraising campaigns will become more sophisticated and you will want to consider very precise queries, but in the beginning, you need to collect and carefully maintain your core supporters. Do not bombard these supporters with requests for funding, but consider distributing an annual or semiannual fundraising letter.

#202. How do I use a mailing list as "currency"?

It is highly unethical to sell or trade a mailing list. However, you can offer to include information from like-minded groups in your mailing. In exchange, those groups should include information from you in their mailings. This is a perfectly acceptable way for your information to reach the mailing lists of like-minded organizations while keeping each group's list private. Establishing clear criteria for accepting this type of cross-promotion is a function of the board of directors. You will find it necessary to turn down most inquiries you receive, but it can be a good way to broaden your coverage, build alliances with other organizations, and ultimately help the other nonprofits in your area.

#203. What is public access television?

Public access television is a form of community-based TV. It has been around for decades, yet it remains a mystery to many organizations. If a cable television provider serves your region, you have a public access television channel. It might be the channel that carries your city or county council meetings or high school athletics.

Your local cable provider will have specific details on how to submit a program. Many parts of the country offer two options: a scheduled slot that occurs every month or week, or a completely random slot that usually ensures your program will make it in, but not at a designated time. From a production standpoint, there is no difference.

As an organization, you will be responsible for all the production and editing. Many communities have groups to assist with public access production, which includes training people to operate cameras and use current editing software.

The audience of public access television is almost entirely local, so if the focus of your nonprofit is heavily local as well, you're reaching out to your key demographic.

#204.   How can my organization use scheduled programming?

As a nonprofit, you may be able to secure a regular slot in the public access schedule. Generally speaking, if the program is geared to all audiences (no profanity, etc.), and there is space in the schedule, you will have an equal chance of securing a slot as any other organization or individual.

Committing your organization to a regular production is a huge step and one you do not want to take on until you have enough support. If there is interest in using this wonderful community resource, talk with your local cable provider and other programmers to get their opinions on how effective their programs have been.

#205.   How can my organization use random or drop-off programming?

Most public access channels allow program material to be dropped off at established times for broadcast when there is nothing else scheduled. Such material must be in a "plug and play" format. The station engineer should be able to start the program you dropped off at the business office and then walk away, allowing it to run without any further adjustment. Do not expect any production assistance with this option. If there is a mistake on the disk you deliver to the station, that mistake will go out to all the cable subscribers. This is an option if you lack the production ability to put together a regularly scheduled program.

Chapter 12

THE 1023 AND BEYOND

#206. What is Form 1023?

Form 1023 is your application for tax-exempt status. It is made up of eleven parts that you must fill out with the supplementary information requested. Following is a list of the parts of Form 1023:

Part I. Identification of Applicant: Fill in the organization's name, mailing address, Employer Identification Number, and other relevant information.

Part II. Organizational Structure: Identify how your organization is set up (corporation, limited liability company, unincorporated association, or trust) and provide supporting documents.

Part III. Required Provisions in Your Organizing Document: When you wrote the articles of incorporation, you included two specific clauses to comply with IRS requirements. You will need to refer to those clauses, which (1) define the purpose of your nonprofit, and (2) outline what happens to excess funds (those remaining after all the bills are paid) when the organization closes.

Part IV. Narrative Description of Your Activities: Write a description of your organization's activities.

Part V. Compensation and Other Financial Arrangements with Your Officers, Directors, Trustees, Employees, and Independent Contractors: If you are paying anyone for services directly related to the operation of your organization, identify them here and give details of their compensation.

Part VI. Your Members and Other Individuals and Organizations That Receive Benefits from You: This part contains a series of three yes or no questions.

Part VII. Your History: There are two yes or no questions in this part.

Part VIII. Your Specific Activities: This series of questions asks you to go into detail about how your nonprofit operates.

Part IX. Financial Data: Using the chart, outline your finances for the current tax year and the three previous years. If your nonprofit was formed within that time frame, you must make good-faith estimates regarding your future budget. Rules allow a new organization that may not have a financial history to include its current budget, and two projected "accounting periods" (understood to be years) as evidence that it intends to be a public charity rather than a private foundation.

Part X. Public Charity Status: Specify whether you are a private foundation or a public charity.

Part XI. User Fee Information: This section determines your fee for submitting Form 1023.

In addition, there are eight schedules. You will only have to complete the one(s) that apply to your nonprofit.

#207. How do I fill out Part IV of Form 1023?

The first three parts of Form 1023 are straightforward and self-explanatory. The challenge for every group applying for tax exemption is Part IV, the narrative.

Begin with a few short paragraphs explaining what your organization is and what it does. Let the reader know in the first or second sentence that the group was formed "for exclusively charitable and educational purposes."

Offer a brief history of the organization, focusing on activities that point to the requirements of a 501(c)(3) organization. If you are applying as an educational organization, identify activities that support that application. Only discuss projects that are actually taking place or are planned.

You can quote portions of the IRS code in your narrative and then explain how your organization complies not only with the spirit of the law but also with its language. The audience for this narrative is the IRS. The personnel who read this want you to succeed, but they must be certain that your organization complies with every element of the law.

Avoid any mention of restricted activities. You need to show how your organization adheres to the narrow definitions in the Internal Revenue Service code. Also, avoid any suggestion of lobbying. If your organization's mission is to offer after-school tutoring to inner-city kids, stay with that discussion; do not drift into suggestions about proposed changes in the federal or state budget that may affect your program. Although individual members of your organization may be directly involved in lobbying one side or the other, you, as an organization, must stay clear of any such activities.

Similarly, do not suggest that your work will help the members of your organization. The organization must help the community. Your members are a part of the community, but the focus cannot be on them. If you put in language to the effect that the membership is going to be a primary beneficiary of the group's work, you probably won't qualify for tax exemption.

A nonprofit organization may not participate to any substantial extent in business activity unrelated to its purpose and mission. As you describe your business activities, show how those activities directly relate to your purpose and exist only to support your charitable goals.

#208.   **What attachments do I need?**

Every activity or program you identify in the narrative must have some form of supporting documentation. Each time you refer to an event, consider what resources you can use as supporting attachments. If you have a schedule of ongoing events, include a copy of your monthly calendar. If you have press clippings, include copies. If you maintain a monthly newsletter detailing current and planned activities, send a representative sample as part of your narrative.

Explain clearly what your organization is doing, provide documentary evidence of your activities, and show how your program complies with the letter of the IRS code. By showing why and how you will follow any reasonable interpretation of that code, you make the case for why you should qualify for tax-exempt status.

#209. What financial data should you include with Form 1023?

The budget you include with your application will assist the IRS in further understanding any details you discussed in the narrative. If your group claims to be operating as a public charity, your budget clearly indicates how much of your income is from public sources. No particular format is required, so use whatever system you have set up and include it as an attachment to the application.

If you have been in existence for a short time and do not yet have a multiple-year budget, expand upon what you do have to show how you plan to operate in five years. The main point is to show that you expect continued and increased funding from public sources and that your budget corresponds to the narrative.

#210. What is the user fee for Form 1023?

One of the first questions most organizations ask when they consider making an application for federal tax exemption is "How much does it cost?" The user fee, or the money the IRS charges to accept and review your application, is completely separate from any fee you negotiate with a tax consultant or lawyer in the preparation of the application.

The user fee is due with the application. If the fee is not included, the application will not be reviewed. The fee is nonrefundable; if your application is rejected or you receive a determination other than what you wanted, the fee will not be returned. There are actually two possible fees, depending on what your gross receipts are or what you project them to be over the next four years.

1. If your organization's gross receipts will be $10,000 or more, your user fee will be $850.
2. If your organization's gross receipts are under $10,000, your user fee will be $400.

These were the amounts as of the publication date of this guide, but they may change. The IRS will cross-reference your revenue projections with your user fee to make sure you paid the correct amount.

#211.   **What is the advance ruling process?**

This process allowed a new organization that lacked years of documentation to obtain a favorable determination and then have five years to show that it was a publicly supported organization. At the end of those five years, the organization had to file another form showing that it met the standards and should be granted a final determination.

As of 2008, the advance ruling process was eliminated. You still need to plan for and show in your budget that your organization is indeed a public charity. If your organization is relatively new, and thus has not been receiving public funds for several years, you need to show in your narrative and in your budget that you can reasonably expect to be publicly supported. You must meet that one-third threshold before the IRS will accept that you are a public charity.

With your sixth taxable year, you must file your yearly Form 990, showing you meet the public support test.

#212. **What supplementary materials should I include?**

There are no rules on this. You must include the formally required elements, but any supplementary information can be included or excluded at your discretion. Keep in mind that you have one chance to introduce your organization to an IRS agent who has never heard of you or your group. In the course of that introduction, you must clearly document the fact that your organization understands the language governing a nonprofit organization.

The agent will be familiar with Form 1023. It details your financial history and is, to some degree, presented on good faith by all parties involved. The supplemental materials should drive home the fact that you are a viable organization with media coverage, regular recorded meetings, classes open to the public, an engaged and supportive membership base, and a community already aware of and committed to supporting you in a number of ways.

The reason you want to have a clear media strategy and cultivate good contacts in the local press is to increase your media coverage so that you can use samples of that coverage to document your activities to the IRS. These early budgets and program samples can help show that you are a viable group, doing what you say you are doing.

There is also no definitive rule on how much assembled material to include with your application. Any activity that you reference in your narrative or any line item in your budget that has a real, tangible result will help your case.

#213. **Should I consider an outside review?**

The 1023 application is a complicated form, not the least because of the IRS's interest in making absolutely certain that any organization applying for tax exemption meets all the requirements and understands the responsibilities of a nonprofit organization. Because this form is so difficult—particularly if you tackled the application yourself—it's a good idea to ask an expert to review all the materials before you submit them.

#214.   **Should I consult a tax professional?**

If you are nervous about navigating the complex world of federal nonprofit status, it may be worth hiring a tax lawyer. Any competent lawyer whose area of specialty includes nonprofit organizations can help you through the entire process, from filing incorporation documents to drafting bylaws to completing Form 1023. Your lawyer will know what the IRS expects to see, and he can make sure you have all the materials you need. Expect to work closely with him. He may know the tax code, but he also needs to know everything about your organization—who your organization serves, where you expect funding to come from, how you will use the funds, and countless other details. The more he knows about your organization, the fewer questions the IRS will have about your application and the more smoothly the application process will go.

#215.   **What should the application packet include?**

The application packet must include everything the IRS expects to see. Each item should be clearly marked with the organization's name, mailing address, and Employer Identification Number. Do not send loose clippings or half-completed forms. The following is the basic list of what you need to include:

- An envelope containing the check for the user fee. Make your check out to "United States Treasury" for either $400 or $850.
- The two-page Form 1023 Checklist, found at the end of Form 1023. You need to tell the IRS which Form 1023 schedules you are filing as well as where to find your organization's purpose and dissolution clauses.

- Form 2848, Power of Attorney and Declaration of Representative. If your organization is represented by a tax professional, this form identifies her and states your relationship.
- Form 8821, Tax Information Authorization. Fill out this form if you want the IRS to discuss your application with a third party. Most groups will never file this form, so you probably do not have to worry about it.
- Expedite Request. If you are asking the IRS to expedite review of your application, you can submit this request in the form of a letter. Ask an outside expert to review this letter to ensure it meets your needs and those of the IRS.
- Form 1023
- Articles of Organization. If you are incorporated, this should be the articles of incorporation. Otherwise, submit your constitution, articles of association, or other governing document. Bylaws alone are not enough. Articles of incorporation should clearly show that they have been filed with the proper state authority. The IRS usually asks for two signatures on the governing instrument of an unincorporated association.
- Bylaws. These should be signed and dated.
- Form 5768. Fill out this form if the organization has decided to make expenditures to influence legislation under section 501(h) of the Internal Revenue Code.
- Actual financial data, including income statement(s) and a recent balance sheet, if the organization has had any financial activity.
- A two-year projected budget, showing both expected sources of income and anticipated expenses. Sometimes the IRS asks for a projected budget even when the applicant can provide a full year of actual financial data.

Here are a few other items to include in your packet:
- Printed materials describing the history of the organization, its activities, and its plans for the future

- Sample copies of your organization's newsletter if you publish one
- Any materials prepared for members, membership application forms, promotional materials, sample membership certificates or identification cards, sample copies of members-only publications, and so on
- Copies of newspaper clippings, transcripts of interviews, and so on
- Any documentation you have regarding grant monies
- A schedule of events, showing where and when your organization has held informational or other events during the past twelve months; include approximate attendance figures
- If you have a scholarship or grant program, a description of how potential applicants will hear about your program
- Letters between your organization and potential members or board members, letters of appreciation from groups where you have made presentations or otherwise helped out, or even letters from public officials commenting on your efforts
- Advertisements, copies of contracts, rental agreements, leases, and loan agreements involving your organization
- Copies of federal, state, or local legislation, if any, regarding the creation or continued existence of your organization
- Resumes of board members and/or key employees
- Independent appraisals of assets the group is renting or purchasing

#216. What kind of response will I receive from the IRS?

After submitting the application, you can expect a letter from the IRS in about eight weeks acknowledging the receipt of your application. Usually the letter will ask you for additional information. This is not a cause for alarm. If you had a tax professional prepare your application, she can help you with this stage. If you have not had anyone review your application, this is a good time to reconsider that decision. If there are questions, carefully prepare a written response.

If there are ten or fewer questions, you are probably in very good shape and you can expect approval of your application without additional hassle. If, on the other hand, there are fifteen or more questions, there may be problems with your application. Regardless, answer all questions truthfully and in detail and submit the answers to the IRS within the deadline stated in the letter.

#217. **Can I call the IRS about my application?**

The letter will give you the name and telephone number of your contact person at the IRS. Call this person and find out exactly what he or she wants to know. Contact people can often be very helpful, and the information they give you can help you focus your response to the letter.

Any telephone conversations you have with your IRS contact person are informational only. The only answers to the written questions that matter are your written responses. Both your organization and the IRS are establishing a paper trail so there are no misunderstandings.

#218. **What is a determination letter?**

In due course, the IRS will send you either a favorable or an unfavorable determination letter. If it is unfavorable for a 501(c)(3) determination, some applicants are offered instead a favorable determination for a 501(c)(4) organization. If it is favorable, you have every right to celebrate. Save this letter. It is very important. Not only does it give you critical information about compliance with the IRS, but your potential funding sources will usually ask you for a copy. Make copies of the determination letter and keep the original in a safe place. Over the life of the organization, you may send out copies of that letter dozens—if not hundreds—of times, so make certain you never lose the original.

#219.   **What do I do if my application is denied?**

There will be situations when the IRS determines that your organization does not qualify for a 501(c)(3) determination, and grants you a 501(c)(4) status as an alternative. They may also deny you without presenting an alternative.

One common problem is that supporting documents are not strong enough. You may believe you qualified as an educational organization, for example, but the material or your narrative didn't support that claim.

If you are not satisfied with the decision, you have the right to appeal within thirty days. The appeal must be initiated by a letter to the IRS Office of Appeals detailing the reasons you feel the decision was not accurate and requesting a conference. The address to send the letter will be on the denial letter you received from the IRS.

If you don't appeal within the thirty-day window from the time the denial was issued, the decision will be considered final. Likewise, if the decision on appeal is not favorable, you have exhausted your options.

If you plan to appeal the decision, consult an attorney familiar with the IRS appeal process. The stakes are high and the possible details so extensive that it is best to seek such consultation.

#220.   **What is the importance of liability insurance?**

One reason groups decide to incorporate is to give the individuals involved—owners in a for-profit or board members in a nonprofit—some degree of personal protection from liability. Unfortunately, this does not protect the board as an entity from lawsuits that might be filed over any number of issues, completely apart from financial or fiduciary responsibilities.

Board members can still be exposed to lawsuits. A board member can be named as a defendant if a lawyer decides to name anyone and everyone involved with the organization.

As soon as your organization feels it is necessary, purchase directors and officers liability insurance (D&O insurance). One way that a nonprofit can protect its directors and staff is via the indemnification provision in its bylaws. Although such indemnification is allowed to some extent by all states, it may not be available if the organization simply cannot sustain the losses.

#221. What is "good faith"?

Lawyers often use the term good faith to describe how board members must act at all times in order to avoid lawsuits related to their duties on the board. In general, as long as each board member individually meets his or her fiduciary responsibilities as well as possible (acting in good faith), lawsuits against individual board members for the handling of board affairs can be minimized. The board must also, as a group, understand its duty to act in good faith and operate responsibly to minimize the threat of lawsuits.

In addition, you must maintain transparency in all financial dealings. People involved in the organization at any level should be able to see and understand exactly what you are doing and why you take the actions you choose.

#222. How can my organization minimize risk?

Create operating policies that clearly forbid questionable activities. These policies must be taken seriously.

It is impossible to guarantee that no one will ever bring suit against the group, but deliberate risk management is essential. This is why you must have a clear set of bylaws to govern how all decisions will be made.

Your organization should state how a group member should conduct himself while representing the group. A high priority for every nonprofit must be to recruit and retain effective board leaders who accept their responsibility to do a conscientious job. Board members must do their utmost to uphold the overall health of the organization and minimize the potential for lawsuits.

The board should establish and diligently follow rules and procedures governing its operations. The minutes of the board meetings should demonstrate that the board consistently exercises due diligence and seriously considers the consequences of important actions in advance. These minutes and other important organizational documents should be readily available for periodic reviews and updates.

To reduce the risk of lawsuit, and as a matter of personal financial security, each board member must:

- Ensure that the organization is operating within 501(c)(3) guidelines
- Accept the board's legal responsibility to protect the group's assets
- Confirm all major contracts with formally recorded board authorization
- Attend board meetings
- Require a thorough debate on controversial or complicated issues
- Exercise sound judgment even when relying on the accuracy and integrity of others (including areas of special competence)
- Avoid any conflict of interest or appearance of conflict of interest

If a board member is connected in any way to a business transaction with a friend's group, the board must be prepared to demonstrate clearly that fairness was maintained.

Never assume that actions are acceptable simply because the group agreed to them. Likewise, do not rely on the president of the board to know what is appropriate and what is not. As a member, you must be satisfied with each action. It's that important.

#223. **What kind of employment issues do nonprofits face?**

The overwhelming majority of lawsuits filed against nonprofit organizations involve issues related to employment. The specific issue may involve discrimination in the hiring or termination process, harassment, payment issues, or another area. More often than not, lawsuits are brought by people who feel they have no other recourse.

#224. **What is directors and officers insurance?**

Although the fact that your organization is incorporated with the state protects your board from the financial liability of the organization, it does not protect them from legal actions that might be brought against them. For that protection, you need to carry D&O insurance for every board member.

D&O insurance protects nonprofit organizations when claims arise from allegations that nonbodily damage resulted from policy decisions made by the board of directors or from actions by the board and volunteers based on those policies. These damages are considered to be the result of wrongful, intentional acts rather than mere negligence. About 90 percent of D&O suits against nonprofit organizations are employment related. These lawsuits include wrongful termination, sexual harassment, and age, sex, or race discrimination. Most of the remaining 10 percent of D&O suits deal with allegations that the board of directors committed a breach of its fiduciary duty to appropriately use and protect the organization's assets and resources. The accusations may be directed against the entire group or against individual members of the group and may come from donors, concerned citizens, or government officials.

#225.   **What is employee insurance?**

Some organizations choose to purchase another level of protection specifically designed to address negligence on the part of the organization. These policies have many names, but they are often bundled with the D&O insurance policies and are intended to protect board members against lawsuits brought by current or former employees.

A very important consideration that your insurance carrier can more fully explain involves the limitations of most policies that address employee lawsuits. A general liability or D&O policy protects the organization as long as there was coverage when the alleged incident took place, even if the policy was later discontinued for whatever reason. However, policies that protect against employee lawsuits must have been in effect when the incident took place, and they must still be in effect when the lawsuit is filed.

This is particularly relevant in overtime pay lawsuits and certain types of harassment, where the employee has many years to file a legal case. The insurance must be retained or the organization will be fully exposed with no possible way to collect if it is determined that they are indeed at fault and are required to pay.

Maintaining an open-door policy throughout the organization and keeping your financial affairs as transparent as possible will help eliminate many of the risks that insurance policies are designed to handle. Still there is nothing you can do to protect your nonprofit from someone who is intent on bringing a lawsuit against you or the organization if his sole purpose is to disrupt your operations. This is why D&O insurance is a good idea.

#226. What is general liability insurance?

The moment your organization owns or leases anything of real value (such as property, structures, or even a vehicle), you need to consider buying insurance. General liability insurance provides protection from claims arising from bodily or property damage considered to result from simple negligence. Every group is at risk of such claims. For example, a volunteer's actions could injure or damage another person or someone's personal property. A person could be hurt or experience property damage while attending an event on your property. The injured party might claim your organization or an individual was negligent or reckless. Liability insurance will pay for legal defense and any financial judgment incurred. To protect assets that belong to the group, such as office equipment and merchandise inventory, you may need to buy personal property or physical damage insurance coverage.

#227. How do I maintain a sense of perspective about insurance needs?

Any discussion about insurance will inevitably drift to every possible worst-case scenario. We live in a highly litigious culture. However, as a start-up nonprofit, you need to maintain a sense of perspective and differentiate between the risks you may face and the risks that do not apply to your situation. Until you have employees or own property, you may be able to satisfy your coverage with basic D&O insurance.

228. What types of specific situation insurance might I need?

That depends on the type of services or programs you offer. Many venues that regularly rent their facilities to community organizations will require the renter to carry public-assembly or mass-gathering insurance. Cities may require a similar type of policy if you are planning to use a public park or public facility for your event.

If your organization is planning to hold events on public property such as a city park or street, meet and get to know the people in your city's or county's risk management office. These people are responsible for protecting the city from any liability, and they are the ones who will require you to carry insurance policies. More often than not, the fact that you are a nonprofit has little bearing on their concerns, but it will be important when you take out a policy with an insurance carrier.

If you are planning any type of festival that will have booths and food, require each vendor to carry insurance and name your organization as the insured party. You can present this when you go through the permitting process to hold your event.

These policies protect your organization as well as any municipal jurisdiction from damages that may result if someone gets hurt during the event and decides to seek a legal remedy. These policies are usually written to cover up to $5 million per incident.

#229. How does the Volunteer Protection Act affect my organization?

The Volunteer Protection Act of 1997 provides that a volunteer meeting certain criteria shall not be liable for damage resulting from "simple negligence" while performing authorized volunteer activities for a 501(c)(3) organization. The definition of a volunteer as an "individual performing services without receipt of compensation (other than reasonable expense reimbursement) or any other thing of value in lieu of compensation in excess of $500 per year" also includes directors and officers.

Although the Volunteer Protection Act protects volunteers from being held liable for damage caused by their acts of "simple negligence," it does not protect against liability for damage caused by "gross negligence." The line of demarcation between "simple negligence" and "gross negligence" is difficult to determine, both practically and legally. Other aspects of the act's provisions, including the concept of "authorized" activities and "things of value in lieu of compensation," are also somewhat open to interpretation. In addition, the act does not actually prohibit lawsuits against volunteers. It was primarily intended to protect the assets of directors, officers, and volunteers by making the nonprofit sponsor the one held accountable for damage resulting from a volunteer's simple negligence.

#230. What are the first steps to take when changing a for-profit to a nonprofit?

Any change to your basic structure that moves your current for-profit business into the nonprofit sector will require intense analysis. The core reasons that prompt the change must go far beyond your current cash flow or profit and loss statement. The relationship your business has with the community you serve may lend itself to a nonprofit status. You may receive a certain level of public support and your business may have an honest focus that lines up with the IRS requirements for nonprofit status.

If you are considering transforming a for-profit business into a nonprofit organization, there is a good chance you have heard the term nonprofit but have never had any reason to learn exactly what is involved in starting and running one. The first step is to gather as much information on the topic as you can find. Talk to people who are involved in running nonprofits in similar fields, read books, and research websites, including the IRS site.

#231.   How does funding play into changing from a for-profit to nonprofit?

For anyone considering a conversion from for-profit to nonprofit, the sources of income are crucial. The decision to convert from a for-profit to a nonprofit will rest on where your funding comes from (the charitable question), and you must be absolutely certain that all expenditures are in absolute compliance with the rules governing nonprofits. Unlike a start-up nonprofit, a for-profit business already has income sources and expenditures, which may not align with the rules governing nonprofits.

#232.   Can I change to a nonprofit to avoid income tax responsibilities?

If you are considering changing from a for-profit to a nonprofit to avoid any corporate income tax responsibilities, stop immediately. You are on a dangerous path. You are hardly the first person to come up with such an idea, and your intentions will become very clear to any IRS personnel who review your application.

If you try to falsify your financial documents to meet standards you believe will prove your case, you will dig yourself deeper into a legal hole. When your charade is exposed (as it surely will be), it will cast a long shadow over the entire nonprofit community, which has been living and working by the rules all along. It is hard enough to maintain the cash flow necessary for nonprofit organizations to do their essential work without having to answer for people who are trying to scam the system.

#233.   Can becoming a nonprofit help my organization with financial difficulties?

If your business is struggling financially, becoming a nonprofit is not going to change very much. A for-profit organization operates very much the way a nonprofit does, except that no individual may benefit financially from the work of the organization. If your supplies are costing too much, your expected fees for service are not meeting projections, or you are having trouble making payroll, becoming a nonprofit will not help you. If your business plan and projections are not working, adjust them to current economic realities instead of scrapping them with an eye toward reorganizing the entire company.

#234. How does the twenty-seven month rule apply to switching from a for-profit to nonprofit?

If you have not been in business for twenty-seven months, you may be able to more easily switch from a for-profit to a nonprofit. From the viewpoint of the IRS, you are simply a business paying your corporate taxes like anyone else.

The first question, provided you are indeed within the window, is what you indicated when you incorporated with the state. Remember, all your documentation regarding incorporation is a state issue, not federal. You will most likely need to file extensive articles of amendments, essentially reforming your organization to comply with the nonprofit standards as opposed to the for-profit ones you originally created.

Either you or your attorney needs to make an initial inquiry to your state secretary of state or the office where you filed your original articles of incorporation to determine the process you need to follow to make the switch at the state level. Get the names of each person you speak with, and prepare a follow-up note to reiterate the issues discussed.

Be certain that everything you do is in writing. Telephone calls are fine for general questions, but they are worthless in establishing a paper trail.

If you are within the twenty-seven-month window, you must still check with the office in your state where you filed the articles of incorporation and make the necessary changes to your core corporate documents. You may have to file articles of amendment, but you will probably also have to explain in detail how and why the original circumstances have changed and why your organization is now seeking incorporation as a nonprofit. It may be possible that you made a mistake in filing the initial articles of incorporation, which can be rectified with a letter of explanation and amended articles.

If, on the other hand, you incorporated as a traditional for-profit business, have been operating as a for-profit business for twenty-seven months or longer, and now decide you are really a nonprofit charitable organization, you will face an uphill struggle. It is highly unlikely your group will be able to gain a favorable decision, and it may be time to seek an alternative route to gaining nonprofit status.

#235. How do business plans need to change when switching from a for-profit to nonprofit?

To change from a for-profit to a nonprofit may require adjusting how your entire organization views itself and its place in the community. You will have to re-examine a number of the core assumptions that very likely motivated you when you started your for-profit business. One of the largest sticking points may be your interest (or your investors' interest) in making money, and this means rethinking your business plans.

You must also completely rethink what you do and why you are doing it. You need to reconsider why you are even in existence. The IRS is very clear on the basic criteria that any organization must meet before it obtains a favorable nonprofit determination. Those criteria do not suddenly change to accommodate someone who is interested in turning a for-profit business into a nonprofit—in fact, you can expect a narrow interpretation of the rules and more pointed questions or a need for clarification.

#236.   What operational changes need to take place?

You will have to identify the internal changes you adopted to qualify as a nonprofit. Simply deciding you are a nonprofit is not enough. Your entire organization must meet the criteria for a nonprofit, including how you are organized and whether anyone owns shares or stock or, in any way, expects to see a return on some sort of investment in the organization. These elements will immediately disqualify your group from attaining nonprofit status, so you must make the necessary operational changes within your organization as soon as possible.

#237.   What revenue changes need to take place?

You must show clearly that your base of financial support is the public. This is not going to be easy. The entire premise of a functioning for-profit business is exactly the opposite of a nonprofit.

For example, consider a coffee shop whose revenue is derived from the sale of tangible goods (namely, coffee and food). The profits generated go to the owner. However, the shop hosts open mic nights and allows local performers to use the space for concerts, in addition to holding educational workshops and music lessons. There is a significant level of public support from patrons paying to see performers, but it is not the primary income for the business.

As a nonprofit, it becomes essential to show that the public support for the concerts, educational workshops, and musical instrument lessons is responsible for keeping that portion of the facility, designated as a nonprofit organization, functioning. You must show, through budgets and bank statements, that the profit from that portion of the facility (which is the nonprofit portion) is returned to the organization, never to any individual.

#238. How do I form a nonprofit within my current organization?

One option that has been implemented successfully is to form a new nonprofit within your existing for-profit business. The purpose of this new organization would be to carry out the elements of your overall mission that fall within the parameters of the IRS tax-exempt regulations, even as you operate the for-profit business. Although it is certainly not a guarantee of success, this model has been followed by a number of organizations around the country that did indeed receive their IRS determination letters.

There are many issues to be addressed. You'll need to explain how one space can be used by two different entities and who takes financial responsibility for the many items delivered to the businesses and possibly shared in the normal course of doing business.

A slight modification of this option is to form a parallel 501(c) (3). The new nonprofit could be financially supported, at least initially, by its for-profit parent. This particular model allows current investors to remain fully involved. Although they will no longer be seeing a financial reward, they may become contributors to the new nonprofit. As such, they will be able to deduct all or part of that contribution (depending on the particulars) from their personal income tax liability.

The parallel organization cannot be a carbon copy of the existing for-profit business. It must be organized as a self-sustaining nonprofit, following all the rules and requirements of any other 501(c)(3).

#239. When and why should I start from scratch?

Consider starting from scratch if you are contemplating a change after you have been incorporated longer than twenty-seven months or if you have other complicating factors that make the change to a nonprofit too difficult or impossible. The huge advantage of starting another organization is that you will already have the contacts, the infrastructure, and possibly the staff. You and your organization will also have the most valuable commodity to bring to the table: real-world experience in running a business and working with people.

#240. **Do I need to change my organization's name?**

If the decision is to start over, you may have to change the name of the organization or adjust it so that it is recognizable but clearly different. Think of yourselves as completely reorganizing, which may unfortunately mean a name change if you have well-established name recognition in the community.

#241. **What impact will the change have on my organization?**

Businesses and organizations change their names and, at times, endure entire makeovers. Sometimes the transformation is due to marketing plans or changes in leadership, or perhaps to define more accurately the organization's place in the community.

In reality, apart from those directly involved in the governance of an organization and those who have been financial contributors, no one really pays attention to these details. With good publicity you may be able to mark the name change without changing the public perception of your organization.

Far more complicated than a name change will be the need to fundamentally change the organizational/corporate structure of a for-profit business to comply with both the letter and spirit of the IRS code as it pertains to nonprofit organizations. A board of directors will become the governing body, which can mean that the former owner or manager will no longer have the final word on operational decisions. Rather than having a revenue stream based on the sale of goods and services, revenue will now show public support in any of the forms discussed elsewhere in this book.

Finally, you will need to eliminate the concept of expecting a return on investments made in a business. People will be encouraged to make contributions and donations to the organization, but they can never do so expecting to see a financial return as with an investment in a for-profit company.

Chapter 13

TRIBAL NONPROFITS AND SAMPLE DOCUMENTS

#242. What are tribal nonprofit organizations?

In 1982, the U.S. Congress passed the Indian Tribal Governmental Tax Status Act, which was made part of the Internal Revenue Service and recognized as Section 7871 of the IRS Code. Section 7871 treats tribal governments as state governments for a variety of tax purposes. One of these purposes is to allow tribal governments (and their political subdivisions) to receive tax-deductible donations as do nontribal 501(c)(3) organizations.

As more federally recognized tribes continued to open business ventures employing thousands of individuals and generating millions of dollars for local economies, Congress decided to include basic information that will assist tribes with their planning should they decide to use Section 7871 of the IRS Code.

Individuals working with tribes or organizations in some way affiliated with federally recognized tribal governments and interested in forming a nonprofit organization on reservations may contact the First Nations Development Institute for further information and assistance. For more information on this topic, see their website: *www.firstnations.org*.

#243.   **What is section 7871?**

Generally, foundations and public charities fall under Section 501(c)(3) of the Internal Revenue Code. For tribal governments, however, the Indian Tribal Governmental Tax Status Act of 1982 is recognized as an appropriate legal, political, and economic means for Indian nations to establish, regulate, and control philanthropic activities within their communities. This act, codified as the Internal Revenue Code (IRC), §7871, treats tribal governments as state governments, allowing tribal governments, their political subdivisions, or any tribal governmental fund, to receive tax-deductible contributions.

Establishing tax-exempt tribal governmental organizations under IRC §7871 allows tribes to maintain a greater degree of sovereignty than they would under the more customary 501(c)(3) designation. The U.S. Supreme Court has held that Indian nations possess a status higher than states. Thus, the more traditional 501(c)(3) designation subjects Indian nations (and their political subdivisions) to the oversight of the offices of state attorney generals, where jurisdiction over "expressly public and charitable purposes" is generally housed.

#244.   **What are the effects of 7871 on potential donors?**

Section 7871 of the IRS Code offers many of the same tax benefits for donors as 501(c)(3) nonprofits, for practical tax purposes, meaning: All donations to a 7871 tribe or organization are tax deductible, and foundations can make grants to such organizations. The 7871 organizations establish their own accountability to their donors. The code makes deductibility contingent on the gift's being "for exclusively public purposes."

The 7871 option is encouraged to help potential donors understand what might otherwise appear to be a terribly confusing relationship between the tribes and the state or federal government. The effect of using this section is to make the entire process of donating funds to a tribal nonprofit as easy and as seamless as making a contribution to any other nonprofit in the country. A great deal of confusion still exists with respect to how tribes and the local, state, and federal government bodies interact in their official "government to government" capacity. The 7871 option essentially cuts through a lot of that confusion to help donors understand that their contributions are treated just as they are with other nonprofits, with the full understanding and endorsement of the Internal Revenue Service.

#245. **What are the reporting requirements for tribal nonprofit organizations?**

Reporting requirements are not imposed by the federal government. IRS Section 7871 assumes that tribes, their political subdivisions, and tribal colleges will provide fiscal accountability for charitable contributions, as they manage all finances. However, it is important to donors that their contributions are documented and that fiscal procedures are transparent. It is required practice for 501(c)(3) organizations to acknowledge each donation in writing, to report fiscal activities by submitting reports to the state and federal governments (i.e., 990 Forms), and to forbid any substantial part (i.e., greater than 5 percent) of the organization's budget to contribute to lobbying activities (or any portion whatsoever to political contributions). Because donors are familiar with these requirements, they may be worth considering when creating a tribal restricted fund.

#246. **What is an example of articles of incorporation?**

Sample Articles of Incorporation:

XYZ Nonprofit

Articles of Incorporation

The undersigned, for the purpose of forming a corporation under the nonprofit laws of the State of Washington (RCW 24.03), hereby adopts the following Articles of Incorporation:

Article I

The name of the corporation shall be XYZ Nonprofit.

Article II

The term of existence shall be perpetual.

Article III

The purposes for which the corporation is organized are as follows:

XYZ Nonprofit has been organized to support groups and individuals creating social, economic, and cultural transformation toward long-term sustainability through the production of an annual festival and other activities.

XYZ Nonprofit may therefore seek, apply for, and receive donations, grants, loans, and other funding from individuals, organizations, corporations, government agencies, and others to support and conduct, in any manner, any lawful activities in furtherance of these charitable, scientific, and educational purposes.

Notwithstanding any other provision of these bylaws, XYZ Nonprofit shall not carry on any other activities not permitted to be carried on by: (a) a corporation exempt from federal income tax under Section 501(c)(3) of the Internal Revenue Code of 1954 (or the corresponding provision of any future United States Internal Revenue Law); (b) a corporation, contributions to which are deductible under Section 170(c)(2) of the Internal Revenue Code of 1954 (or the corresponding provision of any future United States Internal Revenue Law); or (c) a corporation under the Washington Nonprofit Corporation Act (RCW 24.03).

Article IV

The name of the Registered Agent of the corporation is
_____. The street address of the Registered Office and
Registered Agent is _____.

The mailing address for the Registered Agent is

_____.

Article V

There shall be five directors serving as the initial Board of
Directors. Their names and addresses are as follows:

Article VI

In the event of the dissolution of the Corporation, the net
assets are to be distributed as follows: to organizations of
similar purposes, as determined by the Board of Directors,
which have established tax-exempt status under section
501(c)(3) of the Internal Revenue Code of 1954 (or the corresponding provision of any future United States Internal Revenue Law).

Article VII

The name and address of each incorporator is as follows:

In witness whereof, each incorporator has affixed his/her
signature on this ____th day of _____.

#247.   **What is an example of bylaws?**

Sample Bylaws:

XYZ Nonprofit

Bylaws (Date) ?
ARTICLE 1—PURPOSES
ARTICLE 2—MEMBERSHIP
ARTICLE 3—DIRECTORS
3.1 General Powers
3.2 Number & Qualifications
3.3 Election & Term of Office

ARTICLE 4—OFFICERS

4.1 Number & Qualifications

4.2 Election & Term of Office

4.3 President

4.4 Vice-President

4.5 Secretary

4.6 Treasurer

ARTICLE 5—COMMITTEES

5.1 Executive Committee

5.2 Other Committees

ARTICLE 6—PROCEDURE

6.1 Meetings

6.2 Notice

6.3 Quorum

6.4 Procedure

6.5 Resignation

6.6 Removal

6.7 Vacancies

ARTICLE 7—ADMINISTRATION

7.1 Fiscal Year

7.2 Books & Records

7.3 Contracts

7.4 Loans

7.5 Checks & Drafts

7.6 Deposits

ARTICLE 8—MISCELLANEOUS

8.1 Offices

8.2 Indemnification

8.3 Amendment

8.4 Dissolution

ARTICLE 1—PURPOSES

XYZ Nonprofit has been organized to support groups and individuals in creating social, economic, and cultural transformation toward long-term sustainability through the production of an annual festival and other activities.

XYZ Nonprofit may therefore seek, apply for, and receive donations, grants, loans, and other funding from individuals, organizations, corporations, government agencies, and others to support and conduct, in any manner, any lawful activities in furtherance of these charitable, scientific, and educational purposes.

Notwithstanding any other provision of these bylaws, the Corporation shall not carry on any other activities not permitted to be carried on by: (a) a corporation exempt from federal income tax under Section 501(c)(3) of the Internal Revenue Code of 1954 (or the corresponding provision of any future United States Internal Revenue Law); (b) a corporation, contributions to which are deductible under Section 170(c)(2) of the Internal Revenue Code of 1954 (or the corresponding provision of any future United States Internal Revenue Law); or (c) a corporation under the Washington Nonprofit Corporation Act (RCW 24.03).

ARTICLE 2—MEMBERSHIP

The Corporation shall have no members.

ARTICLE 3—DIRECTORS

3.1 General Powers

The management and control of the affairs of the Corporation shall be vested in its Board of Directors. Directors shall not be employees of the Corporation, nor otherwise be compensated for their duties except for out-of-pocket expenses as determined by the Board.

3.2 Number & Qualifications

The Board shall consist of not less than five (5) or more than fifteen (15) Directors, the specific number to be set by resolution of the Board. Directors must be at least eighteen (18) years of age. Directors shall be sought who have experience or working interest in areas such as finance, real estate, human resources, event management, and/or possess a specific skill necessary to chair and oversee the Community Committees of the Corporation, and work with Community Committee members to arrive at agreed-upon proposals for presentation to the full Board. This Corporation is committed to a policy of fair representation on the Board of Directors, which does not discriminate on the basis of race, physical handicap, gender, ancestry, religion, or sexual orientation.

3.3 Election & Term of Office

The initial Directors named in the Articles of Incorporation shall serve until the first annual meeting. At the first annual meeting, one-third of Directors shall be elected to one-year terms, one-third to two-year terms, and the remaining Directors to three-year terms. At subsequent annual meetings, Directors shall be elected to three-year terms. The term of office for newly elected Directors shall commence at the succeeding Board meeting. Each Director shall hold office until he or she resigns or is removed or is otherwise disqualified to serve, or until his or her successor shall be elected and qualified, whichever occurs first.

ARTICLE 4—OFFICERS

4.1 Number & Qualifications

The officers shall be President, Vice President, Secretary, Treasurer, and such other Officers and assistant Officers as may be determined by the Board. The same person, except the offices of President and Secretary, may hold any two or more offices.

4.2 Election & Term of Office

The Board at the annual meeting shall elect Officers each year. Each Officer shall hold office until he or she resigns or is removed or is otherwise disqualified to serve, or until his or her successor shall be elected and qualified, whichever occurs first.

4.3 President

The President shall be the principal executive of the Corporation responsible for carrying out the directions and resolutions of the Board. He or she shall preside at all meetings of the Board and Executive Committee. Upon resolution of the Board, and not otherwise, he or she may sign with the Secretary, Treasurer, or any other proper Officer authorized by the Board any deeds, mortgages, bonds, contracts, or other instruments (including acceptances of donations, conveyances, or contributions), except in cases where the signing and executing thereof is expressly delegated by these bylaws to some other Officer or agent of the Corporation, or is required by law to be otherwise signed and executed. The President shall in general perform all duties incident to the office of President and such other duties as may be assigned by the Board from time to time.

4.4 Vice President

In the absence of the President, or in the event of his or her inability or refusal to act, the Vice President shall perform the duties of the President and when so acting shall have all the powers, and be subject to, the restrictions placed on the President. The Vice President shall in general perform all duties incident to the office of Vice President and such other duties as may be assigned by the President or the Board from time to time.

4.5 Secretary

The Secretary shall: (a) keep the minutes of the meetings of the Board; (b) see that all notices are duly given in accordance with the provisions of these bylaws or as required by law; and (c) in general perform all duties incident to the office of Secretary and such other duties as may be assigned by the President or the Board from time to time.

4.6 Treasurer

If required by the Board, the Treasurer shall give a bond, at the expense of the Corporation, for faithful discharge of his or her duties in such sum and with such sureties as determined by the Board. The Treasurer shall: (a) have custody of and be responsible for all funds and securities of the Corporation; (b) receive contributions to the Corporation and receive and give receipts for moneys due and payable to the Corporation from any source whatsoever, and deposit all such moneys in the name of the Corporation into such banks, credit unions, trust companies, or depositors as selected by the Board in accordance with the provisions of these bylaws; and (c) in general perform all duties incident to the office of Treasurer and such other duties as may be assigned by the President or the Board from time to time.

ARTICLE 5—COMMITTEES

5.1 Executive Committee

The Executive Committee shall consist of all Officers of the Corporation. The Committee shall have the power to act on behalf of the Corporation subject to final ratification of its acts by the Board. Any Officer may call a meeting of the Executive Committee.

5.2 Other Committees

The Board may establish and empower such standing Community Committees and ad hoc committees as it deems necessary, and may solicit and approve participation by members of the general public. A Director shall chair every committee. Committee chairs shall perform all duties incident to their office as determined by the President or Board. Committee decisions must be approved by the Board prior to enactment.

ARTICLE 6—PROCEDURE

6.1 Meetings

The annual meeting of the Board shall be held during the winter months for the purpose of electing Directors and transacting such business as may properly come before the meeting. Regular meetings of the Board shall be at least quarterly on a date and time established by the Board. Special meetings of the Board may be called by or at the request of the President, any two Directors, or a majority of paid staff of the Corporation. No business shall be transacted at a special meeting except that mentioned in the notice. All meetings shall be held at the principal office of the Corporation or at such other place within the State of Washington designated by the Board or persons entitled to call a meeting. Attendance at meetings of the Board may, in special situations, be by telephonic or electronic means.

6.2 Notice

Unless otherwise stated in these bylaws, notice of all meetings shall be given to the appropriate Directors and committee members not less than ten (10) days prior to the date of the meeting, by or at the direction of the President, Secretary, or committee chair calling the meeting. Notice for all meetings concerning the removal of a Director or Officer, amendment to these bylaws, or dissolution of the Corporation, shall be given to the appropriate Directors or committee members not less than fifteen (15) days prior to the date of the meeting, by or at the direction of the President, Secretary, or committee chair calling the meeting. Any notice required under the provisions of these bylaws or as otherwise required by law shall be given in person or by mail. If mailed, such notice shall be deemed delivered when deposited in the United States mail addressed as it appears in the records of the Corporation, with postage thereon prepaid.

6.3 Quorum

A majority of members shall constitute a quorum for the purposes of conducting business at any meeting of the Board or any committee designated and appointed by the Board. A quorum once attained shall continue until adjournment despite the voluntary withdrawal of enough members to leave less than a quorum.

6.4 Procedure

All meetings shall be conducted according to a standard parliamentary procedure. The Board shall seek to make decisions through the consensus. If consensus cannot be reached in a reasonable period of time, the President may table the decision until the next meeting or ask that a decision be made by the affirmative vote of not less than 75 percent of those present and eligible to vote. Each Board or committee member shall be entitled to one vote. Members not present may vote by written proxy submitted before or at the meeting. Unless otherwise provided for in these bylaws, the act of those present in person or by proxy at a meeting at which a quorum has been attained shall be the act of the body so meeting. Except upon motion properly passed to conduct an executive session, all meetings of the Board shall be open to the public. Executive sessions may exclude anyone not designated in the motion for executive session, but shall be only for personnel matters, property acquisition, and communication with legal counsel.

6.5 Resignation

Any Director, Officer, or committee member may resign at any time by delivering written notice to the President, Secretary, or appropriate committee chair at the registered office of the Corporation, or by giving oral or written notice at any meeting. Such resignation shall take effect at the time specified therein, or if the time is not specified, upon delivery thereof.

6.6 Removal

The Board may remove any Director, Officer, or committee member if they have knowingly violated the rules and policies of the Corporation or carried out activities without Board authorization that have legal or financial consequences for the Corporation. Such termination may take place at any Board meeting. If removal of a Director is proposed, all Directors shall be notified of the meeting and the cause for the proposed termination.

6.7 Vacancies

A vacancy on the Board or any committee, or in any office, may be filled by approval of the Board for the duration of the unexpired term. If the number of Directors in office is less than the minimum required by these bylaws, a vacancy may be filled by approval of a majority of the Directors then in office or by a sole remaining Director.

ARTICLE 7—ADMINISTRATION

7.1 Fiscal Year

The fiscal year shall be the calendar year or such other period as determined by the Board.

7.2 Books & Records

The Corporation shall keep correct and complete books and records of accounts, minutes of the meetings of the Board and committees having any authority of the Board, and, at its registered office, the names and addresses of the Directors and Officers. All books and records shall be open for public inspection for any proper purpose at any reasonable time.

7.3 Contracts

The Board may authorize any Officer or agent of the Corporation to enter into any contract or to execute and deliver any instruments on behalf of the Corporation.

7.4 Loans

No loans shall be contracted on behalf of the Corporation and no evidences of indebtedness issued in its name unless so determined by the Board. No loans shall be made to any Director.

7.5 Checks & Drafts

All checks, drafts, or other orders for the payment of money or other evidences of indebtedness issued on behalf of the Corporation shall be signed by such Officer or agent of the Corporation in such a manner as determined by the Board.

7.6 Deposits

All funds of the Corporation not otherwise employed shall be deposited to the credit of the Corporation in such banks, trust companies, or other depositories as determined by the Board.

ARTICLE 8—MISCELLANEOUS

8.1 Offices

The principal office of the Corporation shall be located in ABC County of the State of Washington. The Corporation may also have offices at such other places within the State of Washington as its business and activities may require and as the Board may, from time to time, designate.

8.2 Indemnification

The Corporation may indemnify to the fullest extent permitted by Washington State law any person who was or is a party to or who is threatened to be made a party to any threatened, pending, or completed action, suit, or proceeding, whether civil, criminal, administrative, or investigative, by reason of the fact that the person is or was a director, officer, employee, or agent of the Corporation against expenses (including attorneys' fees), judgments, fines, penalties, damages, and any amounts paid in settlement actually or reasonably incurred by him or her in connection with the action, suit, or proceeding. In addition, the Corporation may pay for or reimburse the reasonable expenses of a Director, Officer, employee, or agent of the Corporation who is a party to a proceeding to the extent and under the circumstances permitted by Washington State law.

8.3 Amendment

These bylaws may be amended by a two-thirds vote of the Directors at any meeting of the Board provided all Directors have been notified of this purpose, and that as amended the bylaws shall not contain any provision that permits the Corporation to carry on activities not permitted by a corporation exempt from federal income tax under Section 501(c)(3) of the Internal Revenue Code or the corresponding provision of any future federal tax code, or by a corporation incorporated under the Washington Nonprofit Corporation Act (RCW 24.03).

8.4 Dissolution

The Corporation may voluntarily dissolve and cease to operate upon the affirmative vote of not less than 75 percent of the Directors at any meeting of the Board, provided all Directors have been notified of this purpose. Upon dissolution, any net assets of the Corporation shall be distributed in accordance with the provisions of the Articles of Incorporation.

ADOPTION OF BYLAWS

XYZ Nonprofit Board of Directors on _____ adopted the forgoing bylaws.

_____

Secretary

#248.   **What is a sample budget?**

Sample Budget:

XYZ Nonprofit Community Theater Operation Budget OPERATIONS BUDGET OVERVIEW Fiscal Year 2015					
Earned Revenue		**Expenses**		**Net**	
Concerts	48,500	Concerts	43,860	4,640	
Films	93,600	Films	93,000	600	
Arts in Education	15,950	Arts in Education (balance with $15K in grants earmarked for Arts Education)	17,060	(1,110)	
Rentals	130,500	Rentals	99,800	30,700	
Concessions	37,200	Concessions	16,020	21,180	
Ticketing Fees	34,400	Ticket Handling	24,990	9410	
		Marketing	21,200	(21,200)	
Total Earned Revenue	**$360,150**	**Total Earned Expenses**	**$315,930**	**$44,220**	
Unearned Revenue					
Memberships	46,800	Membership & Donor Marketing	3,100	43,700	
City Funding	10,400		10,400		
County Funding	2,500		2,500		
State Funding	2,000		2,000		
Individual & Business Sponsorships	12,700		12,700		
Monthly Program Guide Sponsors	9,000		9,000		
Earmarked Education Grants	15,000		15,000		
Concert & Film Sponsors	2,500		2,500		
Event Sponsors	22,500		22,500		
Fundraising Events	92,100	Fundraising Events	48,200	43,900	
		Payroll	149,990	(149,990)	

Interest	24	Bank Loan	-	24
		Overhead Other Than Payroll	40,932	(40,932)
Total Unearned Revenue	**$215,524**	**Total Unearned Expenses**	**$242,222**	**$(26,698)**
TOTAL REVENUE	**$575,674**	**TOTAL EXPENSES**	**$558,152**	
			TOTAL INCOME	**$17,522**

#249.   What are some sample mission statements?

Sample Mission Statements:

For a Community Theater

To entertain, inform, and inspire our diverse community through cinema, live performance, and educational programs while preserving the historic XYZ Theater.

For an Arts Festival

The purpose of the ABC Fair shall be to educate and inform the public about choices in personal and community lifestyle through the promotion and preservation of the work of individual craftspersons, artists, artisans, musicians, and performers; displays in a traditional fair setting; psycho-spiritual rejuvenation; and the creation of a public forum encouraging the exchange and discussion of ideas about alternative community organization and the use of economic resources and appropriate technology.

For a Music Support Organization

The purpose of ABC Music is to support acoustic music in the Northwest by fostering a community that nurtures musical growth, creativity, and the appreciation of acoustic music.

For a Community Garden

The mission of Central Community Garden is to enhance the quality of urban life and strengthen community bonds by creating and sustaining an organic garden in Sand Point Magnuson Park that will foster environmental stewardship, horticultural education, rejuvenation, and recreation.

#250. What are some sample job descriptions?

Sample Job Description: Executive Director
Executive Director Position Description
XYZ Nonprofit
Under the direction of the Board of Directors, the Executive Director is responsible for overall management and operation of the XYZ Nonprofit and protection of the organization's financial assets while ensuring compliance with Board directives and applicable grantor, federal, and state requirements.

Essential Duties and Responsibilities

The Executive Director is responsible for overall operations, asset protection, and marketing/public relations for XYZ Nonprofit, a 501(c)(3) nonprofit private research and education corporation. The incumbent also:

Oversees all accounting functions including those necessary for auditing, budgeting, financial analysis, capital asset and property management, and payroll in accordance with generally accepted accounting principles.

Handles all aspects of human resource management for up to ### employees, including but not limited to hiring and termination, developing position descriptions, setting compensation, working with employees.

Interacts with other personnel and organizations, such as the city, state, and other public and private entities.

Is responsible for grants and contracts management including negotiating research agreement terms that reflect the needs of XYZ Nonprofit.

Assists in the development of current and long-term organizational goals and objectives as well as policies and procedures for XYZ Nonprofit operations; establishes plans to achieve goals set by the Board of Directors; and implements policies, subject to approval by the Board of Directors.

Analyzes and evaluates vendor services, particularly for insurance, employee benefits, and management of XYZ Nonprofit funds, to determine programs and providers that best meet the needs of XYZ Nonprofit and makes recommendations to the Board, as appropriate; negotiates services, terms, and premiums and executes contracts with benefit plan providers, supply and service vendors, auditors, and consultants; manages payroll and benefits programs.

Education and/or Experience

No specific education required. However, the Executive Director must possess the previously mentioned skills, knowledge, and qualities, which may result from formal education or at least three years' experience in business, nonprofit operational and financial management, or related areas.

Physical Demands

While performing the duties of this job, the Executive Director is regularly required to sit, stand, walk, speak, and hear. The position requires extensive computer use so the employee must have sufficient hand dexterity to use a computer keyboard and be capable of reading a computer screen. The employee must occasionally lift and/or move up to 20 pounds. Reasonable accommodations may be made to enable otherwise qualified individuals with disabilities to perform the essential functions.

Travel

The Executive Director must be able to travel to attend conferences, training, and other events as required to acquire and maintain proficiency in fulfilling the responsibilities of the position.

Work Environment

The work environment is a small, busy office located in <City>. The noise level in the work environment is usually low to moderate. Reasonable accommodations in the work environment may be made to enable individuals with disabilities to perform the essential functions.

Sample Job Description: Administrative Assistant
Foundation Administrative Assistant Job Description
XYZ Foundation

The XYZ Foundation Administrative Assistant is an energetic, amicable, and highly organized individual who provides key support to the Foundation Director, Foundation professional staff, and the Foundation Executive Committee. The Foundation Administrative Assistant will work independently and with multiple Foundation team and committee members. She or he is a professional in her or his own right, and will be the first face and voice of the Foundation that many donors and prospective donors will encounter. This individual will receive training and will have the opportunity to learn about endowment fund development and the world of philanthropy.

Duties and Responsibilities

- Provide executive-level support as required by the XYZ Director
- Schedule meetings and events
- Send out notices for meetings
- Mail out invitations for events
- Prepare agendas
- Prepare any material needed for meetings or events
- Record the minutes of meetings
- Transcribe and distribute minutes in a timely manner

- Prepare reports and statistical reports, as required by professionals
- Post meeting follow-up as required
- Plan staff events
- Recruit assistance from other Foundation administrative assistants, as needed
- Process Foundation correspondence
- Perform Internet research on current and prospective donors
- Enter data into the database
- Create donor profiles
- Maintain files, database, calendars, and hard-copy files
- Record the assignment of donors and prospects into the database
- Maintain accurate records of contacts in the database
- Serve as a liaison between professional staff, other departments, donors, and prospective donors
- Provide logistical support for projects and special events
- Perform other duties as assigned

Qualifications
- Advanced written and spoken (English) communication and administrative skills; excellent telephone manner
- Computer literacy including MS Office products: Word, Excel, Outlook, PowerPoint; experience with mail-merges and with customer or donor databases
- Exceptional time-management, planning, and administrative skills
- Ability to organize and prioritize workload
- High level of diplomacy, sound judgment, and discretion when dealing with donors, volunteers, and community professionals
- Combined four years of full-time work experience and/or higher education
- High degree of energy, self-motivation, and flexibility

Sample Job Description: Board Liaison
Board Liaison Job Description
XYZ Nonprofit
The Board Liaison performs a variety of high-level administrative tasks, which may include budget preparation, travel arrangements and meeting logistics, scheduling, and reporting and tracking information for senior management. He or she provides direct support to high-level Directors and may support other senior managers, including frequent interaction with all members within the organization, as well as customers, vendors, and business relations. The liaison makes interpretations and recommendations as appropriate. His or her duties are highly confidential and require comprehensive knowledge of XYZ Nonprofit's policies, procedures, and operations. These responsibilities require discretion, judgment, tact, and poise. The incumbent has considerable latitude and flexibility in carrying out assigned tasks.

Communications and Interpersonal Contacts

- Formulate and clearly communicate ideas to others, providing a variety of information to staff and others to assist workflow throughout the organization
- Work and communicate with a diverse group of people, including the Board of Directors, donors, volunteers, the public, and other staff
- Demonstrate professional, positive, and approachable attitude/demeanor and discretion
- Demonstrate sensitivity in handling confidential information
- Coordinate multiple diverse projects with several variables, set realistic deadlines, and manage timelines
- Adapt or modify processes in response to changing circumstances
- Interpret guidelines and analyze factual information
- Resolve routine and complex problems independently, with minimal consultation with supervisor

- Demonstrate common sense, flexibility, and teamwork with the strong ability to exercise independent judgment

Supervision/Financial Oversight
- May supervise administrative staff and/or volunteers, interns, and temporary staff
- Financial responsibilities include budgeting for multiple business units
- May serve as delegated financial authority in a variety of areas, such as arranging for large meetings and committing funds related to such meetings and approving expense reports

LIST OF QUESTIONS

1. Why nonprofits?
2. What is a nonprofit?
3. What are the three main types of nonprofits?
4. What is the difference between a 501(c)(3) and a 501(c)(4) organization?
5. What are the federal nonprofit categories?
6. Do I need an MBA to start a nonprofit?
7. How should a nonprofit first engage the community?
8. How does the Citizens United ruling affect nonprofits?
9. What kind of time commitment does a nonprofit require?
10. Where should I set up my office?
11. When should I first interact with leaders of the community?
12. How do I first assess the local media?
13. How do I introduce myself to the media?
14. How do I introduce myself to the local business community?
15. How should I use Facebook to reach out to the community?
16. How should I use Twitter to reach out to the community?
17. How should I use LinkedIn to reach out to the community?

18. How should I use Flickr to reach out to the community?
19. How should I use YouTube to reach out to the community?
20. Should I reach out to other groups in my community?
21. Should I publicize my nonprofit's first meeting?
22. How should I set up for the first meeting?
23. How should I structure our first meeting?
24. What are the limitations of a nonprofit?
25. What are the reporting requirements for a nonprofit?
26. What is the 20 percent rule, and how does it affect my nonprofit?
27. What are the political rules for 501(c)(4) organizations?
28. Should the organization hire a tax lawyer?
29. What is the twenty-seven month rule and how should the group plan to use it?
30. How many members should serve on the initial board?
31. What qualities should I look for when choosing board members?
32. How should I choose the officers of the corporation?
33. What are the responsibilities of the president?
34. What are the responsibilities of the vice president?
35. What are the responsibilities of the secretary?
36. What are the responsibilities of the treasurer?
37. Should the members of the board of directors be paid?
38. What should be discussed at the first meeting of the board?
39. What are the fiduciary responsibilities of the board?
40. What are articles of incorporation?
41. How do I fill out my articles of incorporation?
42. How do I define the purpose of my nonprofit in order to meet IRS standards?
43. How should I include the plans for dissolution of my nonprofit?
44. Can I amend the articles of incorporation once they're written?

45. Whom should I choose to be the registered agent for my organization?
46. What is the difference between a registered agent and an incorporator?
47. How do I file the articles of incorporation?
48. What address should I use for official nonprofit correspondence?
49. How do I obtain a federal tax ID number?
50. Do I need a state business license?
51. As a nonprofit, is my organization exempt from paying state income tax?
52. Do I need a local business license?
53. Should I apply for a nonprofit mailing permit?
54. What is the purpose of bylaws?
55. How do I clearly convey the status of my organization as a charity?
56. How do I lay out the responsibilities of the board of directors?
57. How should I structure the membership options in my organization?
58. How should I set up standing committees?
59. What is the purpose of the finance/budget committee?
60. What is the purpose of the program committee?
61. What is the purpose of an advisory committee, and should my organization have one?
62. How can I use the bylaws to attract people to my organization?
63. What should be included in a meeting agenda and minutes?
64. What needs to be included in my nonprofit's financial records?
65. What is Form 990-N?
66. How will the recent changes to the 990-N affect my nonprofit?
67. What types of projected revenue sources should I include in my projected budget?

68. Can my nonprofit engage in unrelated business activity?
69. What are capital expenses, and how do they fit into the projected budget?
70. What is depreciation?
71. How should I calculate depreciation for my budget?
72. Should I include projected staffing expenses in my budget?
73. How do I include in-kind labor in my budget?
74. What is an "ideal" budget breakdown for a nonprofit organization?
75. How many "authorized check signers" should my organization have?
76. Is it okay to keep some pre-signed checks in the office?
77. What is a commercial bank?
78. What is a retail bank?
79. What is a credit union?
80. What are savings and loan associations?
81. What is a deposit-only account?
82. What is a certificate of deposit?
83. What is a money market?
84. Should I invite bank representatives to my nonprofit's events?
85. How do I establish my nonprofit's financial credibility?
86. How should I involve my nonprofit's committees in fundraising?
87. How should I involve community volunteers in fundraising?
88. What level of financial support should I expect from board members?
89. Should board members be able to fulfill their financial obligations through in-kind contributions?
90. How can I elicit donations from my existing contacts?
91. How do I establish a history for my organization?
92. What is the common grant application?
93. What is a grant writing association?

94. How much money should we raise from public versus private funding sources?
95. What is government funding?
96. What is foundation funding?
97. What is private funding?
98. How should I structure a comprehensive fundraising campaign?
99. What should be the goal of my fundraising campaign?
100. How should my campaign discuss our intention for the money?
101. How should my campaign discuss our plan for getting things done?
102. What is the difference between a fundraising plan and a fundraising campaign?
103. How do I develop a timeline?
104. How can I use house parties for fundraising?
105. How can I use auctions for fundraising?
106. How can I use benefit concerts for fundraising?
107. How can I use phone banks for fundraising?
108. How do I use direct deposit systems for fundraising?
109. How do I use Kickstarter for fundraising?
110. How do I use Indiegogo for fundraising?
111. How do I use DonorsChoose for fundraising?
112. How many online services should my website provide?
113. How does online fundraising save money?
114. How do I provide a complete online shopping experience?
115. What are some examples of in-kind contributions?
116. Are in-kind contributions tax deductible?
117. What is board development?
118. How should the bylaws influence board development?
119. How should fundraising play into board development?
120. Should I engage a consultant for board development?
121. How do I activate the nominating committee?
122. Should committee membership be a route to the board?
123. What is founders' syndrome?

124. How do I assess the immediate needs of my nonprofit for board development?
125. How do I assess the future needs of my nonprofit for board development?
126. What is a conflict of interest for a board member?
127. What is board governance?
128. Should the board connect with other nonprofits?
129. How do I recruit from other nonprofits?
130. What kind of education should the board receive?
131. How do I make sure the board reflects the diversity of the community?
132. Should the board undergo diversity training?
133. What is an executive director?
134. What are the duties of an executive director?
135. What are the duties of a nonprofit's administrative assistant?
136. What is a board liaison?
137. What is a development director?
138. What is a volunteer coordinator?
139. How do volunteers fit in as staff?
140. How should I recognize volunteers' contributions?
141. How do I recruit volunteers?
142. How should my organization participate in special events?
143. What is the role of an accountant in a nonprofit?
144. What is a program/project coordinator?
145. Should nonprofit staff be compensated?
146. Can compensation be tied to performance?
147. What are the problems with excessive compensation?
148. Why does conflict occur between operations staff and the board?
149. Should staff members attend board meetings?
150. How should board members reach out to staff and volunteers?
151. How can committees help with conflict?
152. How do I define board oversight?

180. Can my mission statement change over time?
181. What is my nonprofit's "vision"?
182. What should the mission statement communicate to the general community?
183. What should the mission statement communicate to the nonprofit funding community?
184. What are my nonprofit's guiding principles?
185. What is the sticky dot exercise?
186. What is the round robin table exercise?
187. Does my nonprofit need a website?
188. How should I select a webmaster?
189. What are the basic tasks of creating a website?
190. What type of content should be on my website?
191. Should my nonprofit have a newsletter?
192. How do I use desktop publishing?
193. What should my newsletter contain?
194. How do I distribute my newsletter?
195. Should my organization have a designated media person?
196. How do I create a press release template?
197. How should I use fairs and community festivals for publicity?
198. How do I set up a booth at a fair?
199. Should my organization sponsor a stage at a fair?
200. How do I create a mailing list?
201. How do I use a mailing list for fundraising?
202. How do I use a mailing list as "currency"?
203. What is public access television?
204. How can my organization use scheduled programming?
205. How can my organization use random or drop-off programming?
206. What is Form 1023?
207. How do I fill out Part IV of Form 1023?
208. What attachments do I need?
209. What financial data should you include with Form 1023?
210. What is the user fee for Form 1023?
211. What is the advance ruling process?

239. When and why should I start from scratch?
240. Do I need to change my organization's name?
241. What impact will the change have on my organization?
242. What are tribal nonprofit organizations?
243. What is section 7871?
244. What are the effects of 7871 on potential donors?
245. What are the reporting requirements for tribal non-profit organizations?
246. What is an example of articles of incorporation?
247. What is an example of bylaws?
248. What is a sample budget?
249. What are some sample mission statements?
250. What are some sample job descriptions?

INDEX